Cap Pistols, Cardboard Sleds & Seven Rusty Nails

A Vermont Boyhood in Happy Valley

Cap Pistols, Cardboard Sleds & Seven Rusty Nails

A Vermont Boyhood in Happy Valley

Alec Hastings

FULL COURT PRESS

Copyright © 2021 Alec Hastings
Published by Full Court Press, c/o Alec Hastings,
400 Curtis Road, Randolph Center, Vermont 05061
All right reserved.

ISBN: 978-0-9982812-1-6

Library of Congress Number: 2021912044

No part of this publication may be reproduced or distributed in any form or by any means, electronic or mechanical, including but not limited to photocopying, recording, scanning, or by any information storage or retrieval system, without written permission from the copyright holder. Requests for permission should be mailed to:

Alec Hastings
400 Curtis Road
Randolph Center, Vermont 05061
alecwhastings@hotmail.com

Book design by Carrie Cook

For additional information about this book, contact:
alecwhastings@hotmail.com

Printed in the USA

… [Our parents] were not afraid to let us… fill our days with our own activities. They loved us for who we were, and they left us to ourselves so that from the time we were old enough to leave the house on foot or on our bikes, we were free, and our time was ours. We were out on our own, exploring… having our own experiences as we advanced from childhood to youth and adolescence and adulthood, glimpsing the inwardness of familiar things and building a treasure house of memory….

— Bruce Coffin, *Among Familiar Shadows*

Other books by this author:

Otter St. Onge and the Bootleggers
Rosie and the Little Folk

This book is dedicated to my wife,
Denise Martin.

Sometimes I call her Cookie and sometimes I call her Didi. Always, I call her my love. She makes a mean chicken soup and a mean pizza, and by "mean," I mean wicked good. She is a fountain of laughter and kindness and fun. I drink her in every day! I am glad and blessed to grow old with her. If I have to leave this mortal coil, let me go with her hand in mine. If the ferryman tells me no, I'll dream it so.

Contents

Preface		11
Prologue	Tarzan and the Tree of Life	17
Map of Happy Valley		24
Chapter 1	No Bigger than a Dime	25
Chapter 2	Dad, Our Sean Connery	39
Chapter 3	Mom, Woman of Mystery	67
Chapter 4	The Millhand and the Teacher	95
Chapter 5	How the Hastings Boys Became Bookworms	123
Chapter 6	"You're Not the Boss of Me!"	137
Chapter 7	Elmer, Buddha of Sugar Hill	149
Chapter 8	The Horrible Three	167
Chapter 9	The Snowsuit	191
Chapter 10	Newton's Law of Gravity in Winter	209
Chapter 11	The Great, Silent Cal State Park Vacation	229
Chapter 12	The Undiscovered Country	245
Epilogue		285
Acknowledgements		293

Preface

For Christmas, 2020 my daughters Calley, Josey, and Katie gave me an unusual gift. They signed me up to write stories on a publishing website called Storyworth. They wanted me to write about my boyhood. With an attempt at humor, I said to Calley, "Is this a present for me or for you?"

I was working on a novel at the time, and though I disguised my question as humor, I succumbed to a moment of selfishness. A voice in my head piped up with its ungenerous two cents: "Now, you'll never finish your novel!" At the time, the novel had become an albatross around my neck, and it had me a little worried. I was still at a point where I liked to finish things I started, and I was alarmed at the thought of a time-robbing distraction that would send the novel onto an unused railroad siding and then perhaps to the Bermuda Triangle.

Luckily, my better self said, "Nonsense! Your daughters are giving you a gift. They're giving you a gift, fool! How about extending your open palm and accepting it graciously?" Encouraged by my better self, I told the ungenerous voice to pipe down. I reversed my foolishness and said with slight embarrassment and sincere gratitude, "Thank you. I think this is a great gift, and it should be a lot of fun."

And to my surprise these words turned out to be true. Writing this book *was* a lot of fun, and it *was* a great gift. That Christmas, I didn't understand the true value of the gift, but bit by bit understanding came. Calley told me I would receive a new writing prompt from Storyworth[1] each week, a question that would launch me on a voyage of remembrance and storytelling. This news made me wonder. Could I depend solely on my own memory to resurrect the past, to tell readers about Happy Valley and the folk who lived there in the two decades after World War II? No. I would need help. I asked my older brother Scott and younger brother Duncan for that help because, clearly, if two heads are better than one, three are better than two, and my brothers might remember things I didn't. They were the only other people still alive who could conjure up the world my daughters wanted to know about.

"I'll be calling you," I told them. "Weekly!" I made a point of emphasizing "weekly" because my

---
[1] As it turned out, I did not use Storyworth to publish this book, but it served its purpose as a catalyst.

Preface

Judging by the shadows and tall flowers, it is a late, summer afternoon, a special time because Uncle Bob and Uncle Rinx have come to visit. We have gathered on the stoop of the old Harvey farmhouse to hear stories (from left, Alec, Dad, Uncle Bob, Great Uncle Rinx, and Duncan).

brothers and I had never talked with each other that often. We were raised in rural Vermont by people often described as laconic and reserved. This description applied particularly to the men we knew, the men we admired. Of course, our male elders were not always closemouthed, but the setting had to be right for conversation to flow. Phones were not conducive to that flow. They were commonplace when we were growing up, but none of the men around us picked up a phone just to "visit."

Stamped by that custom, it seemed awkward, at first, to be making regular calls, but soon I looked forward to them. I enjoyed rifling through our shared memories, and I think Scott and Duncan did too. I realized then the first way in which this Christmas assignment truly *had* become a gift from my daughters. It brought me closer to my brothers. We described for each other, cinematically at times, memorable events and experiences from boyhood. As we did so, the faces and voices, the traits, quirks, and temperaments of those who peopled our past came back to us not as ghostly shadows but as technicolor stars.

This new closeness I felt with my brothers was something good that happened when we talked about Happy Valley, and as our conversations unfolded, another good thing happened. As we excavated the past, held the artifacts and bones of memory up in our outstretched hands, and turned them slowly, looking at them from Scott's angle, from Duncan's, and then mine—sometimes we saw them in a new light. It was as if we were all working on a jigsaw puzzle we had found. Many of the pieces had already been assembled, and much of the picture was visible. We could see enough of Mom and Dad and Gram and Gramp to know pretty clearly who they were. We could see Happy Valley scenes that recalled half-forgotten adventures. We could see the old Harvey farmhouse and the house Dad built, but there were missing pieces, too, and they represented mysteries about how all the pieces interlocked and formed one clear picture. The wonderful thing about this book was that it gave my brothers and me a chance to find some of these missing pieces and learn where they fit.

And so, this is what you have at hand, a collection of stories and anecdotes, an unusual Christmas gift, a picture of Happy Valley and its people. For me, it was a special time and place. Of course, it is easy to see the past through rose-colored glasses, to forget childhood experiences that caused tears, but I don't remember Happy Valley with great affection only because I have forgotten such experiences or because I am just one of those glass-half-full people who doesn't see the world as it really is. I remember that valley fondly because it was home and it was happy, because our parents and grandparents raised us there with love and wisdom, because it was a place where Scott and Duncan and I could roam free and discover the wonders of forest and field. We were lucky. I think all stories about happiness are worth sharing. Here is ours.

Prologue

Tarzan and the Tree of Life

I remember well the thrill of climbing trees when I was a boy. The branches of the first tree I ever climbed were close enough to the ground that I could grab one, swing like a monkey into the foliage, and disappear. The enormous, double-trunked pine across the fence from our Happy Valley home was a bigger challenge. Older brother Scott had already conquered this giant. Not me. Finally, I grew strong enough to grip the ridges of the bark and climb like a timid spider up the great bole of the tree. When I was six feet off the ground, I grabbed the two-by-four Scott had salvaged from a broken sawbuck and wedged into the cleft between the trunks. With my free hand, I reached for the lowest branch and scrambled up. I wish I could say I climbed to the top of the tree that day and stood on a limb like a sailor high in his ship's crow's-nest looking out to a wave-tossed horizon. I didn't. Even so, the view was elevated, and I did gain a new perspective.

I had climbed a lot of trees by the time I met the

real king of the jungle. I saw Tarzan for the first time at the Saturday matinee in Woodstock's Town Hall Theater, and I was almost as smitten as his mate, the scantily-clad Jane. *He* could climb like—well, yeah—like an ape-man! Not only that, he could grab a jungle vine and swing from tree to tree! Jeezum crow! As soon as I got home that afternoon, I scrambled up a tree and prepared to stand on a branch like that sailor, like Tarzan. It was time. Grasping a branch above me, I rose carefully to my majestic height of three feet six inches. I opened my mouth wide enough to show my tonsils and ululated Tarzan's primal cry. Tarzan's baritone yodel came from deep down in his exposed, Olympic swimmer's chest. It reverberated to the far reaches of the cinematic jungle and echoed from the cliffs at the base of a smoking volcano. Sabor the Leopard paused in the hunt. Tantor the Elephant raised his head, and one floppy ear twitched. Tarzan's wordless cry was that of a wild beast, but it said clearly, "I am Tarzan, Lord of the Jungle!" I was disappointed that my own cry did not echo off the hillsides of Happy Valley. It limped a few trees away and vanished. As far as I could tell, no creatures stopped what they were doing. I think Spike, our family mutt, may have barked once. But I felt a kinship with Tarzan. Small as it was, my cry said, "I am here!"

PROLOGUE

Inspired by a new, miraculous invention called television, we re-enacted scenes from the Wild West almost daily. The pine tree Scott and I climbed can be seen behind Duncan. From the left are Duncan, Scott, Jimmy Atwood with Spike the Wonder Dog, and Alec.

I still have a soft spot for that hero of my childhood, that English aristocrat raised by Kali the ape, and I still have my copy of Edgar Rice Burroughs' exciting novel,

Tarzan and the Jewels of Opar[2] I think it must have been one of Dad's books because it was published in 1918, but who knows? Gramp was fourteen when the book was published at the end of World War I, so maybe it was his. Why did Tarzan capture my imagination? That's easy. He was like any hero I revered back then, strong and powerful, something a boy could only dream of being. Did I also feel linked with Tarzan in some primal way when I stood on that tree limb and gazed out over the fields of Happy Valley? Did a spark flare in a forgotten corner of my brain, a corner as unused as my tailbone? Did that sudden light awaken a Paleolithic grandfather and pump his blood into my veins for a time-bending second, and did I see an antelope staring back at me from the grasslands? Yes, yes, in my imagination, yes!

Near or far, the past has fired my imagination for as long as I can remember. Much of this fascination, I owe to Dad. Even today I can remember books he read about our origins: *Man the Toolmaker, The Testimony of the Spade, The Tree of Culture.* We all walk in the footsteps of our elders. It must be a very old

---

[2] Later in life I learned that the public's perception of Edgar Rice Burroughs (and therefore Tarzan) had changed. People came to see his books as racist. As a boy, I saw Tarzan as a hero. The child inside me was saddened when he toppled from his pedestal. I learned that truths can change, heroes can become villains, and Truth is more elusive than I had imagined.

Prologue

impulse by now for us to wonder about our forefathers and mothers, where their footsteps came from, where they were headed. Sometimes I want to jump in H.G. Wells' time machine and say hello to my oldest grandparents, the ones sitting at the roots of our stone-age family tree.

But that is fantasy. I can content myself with ruminations on my recent family, the parents and grandparents I knew only yesterday. For a long time, I was too caught up in my own life to realize my parents and grandparents *actually had childhoods* of their own. When this dawned on me at some point in my evolution from whippersnapper to elder, I became curious and I've been curious ever since. Who *were* my parents and grandparents before my brothers and I came along? As I wrote this book during the Covid-19 pandemic of 2020, I wondered what was it like for Gram and Gramp to come of age when thousands and thousands of their generation were dying of the Spanish flu in 1918. Did Gramp ever drink moonshine during Prohibition? How did Grammy, an orphaned Italian American girl, become a school teacher and meet a Yankee millhand like Gramp? Did Dad work up his courage to ask Mom for a date after seeing her play basketball at Keene State in 1946, or did he meet her in the college library? What new stories would

Gramp's brother, the always entertaining Uncle Rinx, tell if he were still alive?

 Now I am old enough to be asked such questions by my own children. *Cap Pistrols, Cardboard Sleds & Seven Rusty Nails* will do its best to answer at least some of them, to part the curtains of memory and see once again the Land of Oz where my brothers and I grew up, to see the people with whom we lived in the 1950s and '60s. Talking to my daughter Calley recently, I remembered that world anew. At the time, it was the *only* world I knew, a world of continuing adventure where one moment I might be painstakingly removing the hook from the mouth of a trout I had just landed on the bank of Happy Valley Brook, and the next I might be hurtling down the High Road on my bike, already tasting the Hollywood candy bar I would buy at the Watsons' store, already planning to hit a double in softball on the Watsons' lawn. Now, as an elder myself I have seen other worlds, but that first one, the world of my youth, is still as magical in my memory as the slide I found of Dad and me playing the bagpipes on the rim of the Grand Canyon in 1967. Yes, the picture of the past has faded, but if we help the Scarecrow down off his cross of sticks, oil the Tin Man's joints, if we click our heels and make our imaginations one, maybe we can see the Land of

Prologue

Oz again in technicolor, and maybe we will glimpse three brothers, Scott, Alec, and Duncan as the boys they were once upon a time.

◆

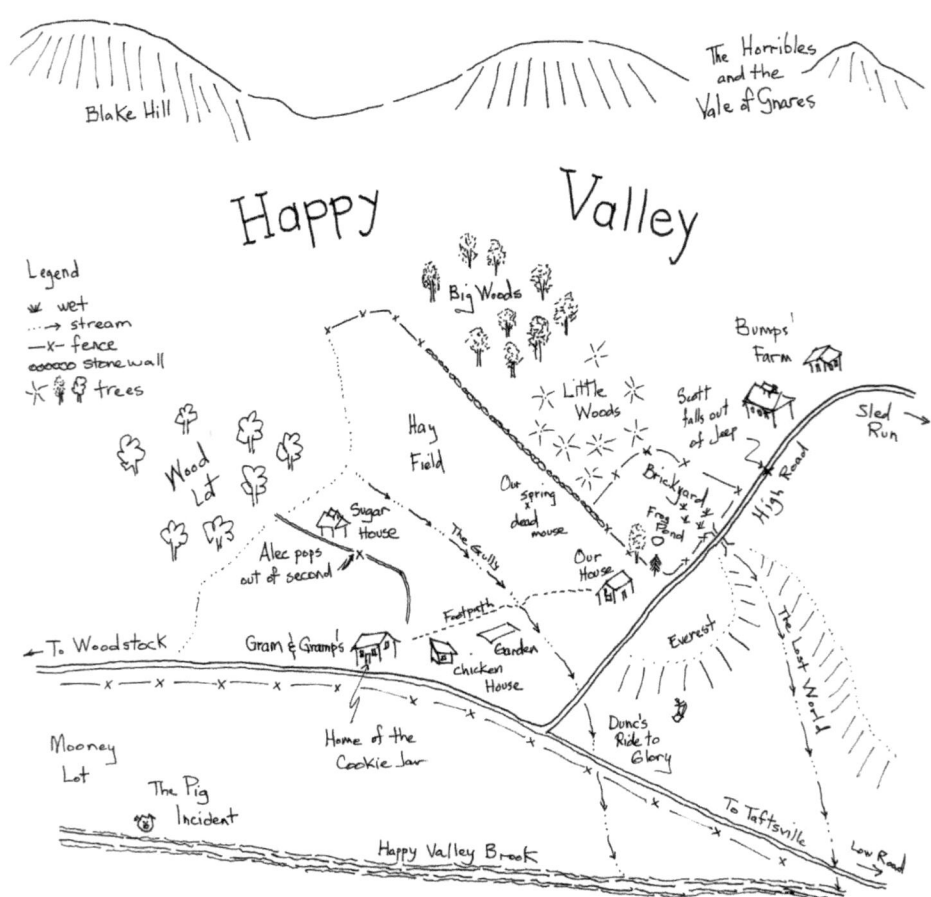

CHAPTER 1

No Bigger than a Dime

Like most people, when I meet someone for the first time, I eventually ask where they're from. Why is this? I suppose it's because we are all children, not only of our parents, but also of the time and place where we grew up. Where we come from has much to do with who we become. And where did the Hastings brothers come from? A place quaintly called Happy Valley. In the 1950s and '60s it was a corner of Vermont no bigger than the Eisenhower dime I often carried in my pocket when Ike had the watch in the White House. Geographically, it is tucked into hobbity hills a mile southwest of Taftsville, a village perched on the banks of the Ottauquechee River at the easternmost boundary of Woodstock. For my brothers and me, its locus is something more. When we were young, Happy Valley was a whole world and an eternity of time.

That post-war decade has often been portrayed as an innocent, idyllic time. Family television series like *The Donna Reed Show, Leave It to Beaver,* and *Father Knows Best* showed an American face that was freshly washed and squeaky clean. Standing by our school desks every morning and placing our hands over our hearts, we Hastings boys pledged allegiance to the United States of America, and we meant it—unless we forgot to pay attention because we noticed the pretty girl in the next row for the first time. Of course, there was a shadow America too. Black people were fighting to free themselves from Jim Crow, fearmongers were promoting the Red Scare, Cold Warriors were rattling the sabers of war, and Michael Harrington's *Other America* was reminding people that life on the other side of the tracks was pretty rough.

We boys began to learn about these troubling events early, especially when Walter Cronkite—"the most trusted man in America"—became the anchorman for the *CBS Evening News*. Dad and Mom watched the news every night. Scott and I must have been absorbing that news too because we competed on a current events quiz show on WCAX-TV when we were in junior high school. Yes, we had our hands over our hearts, but we didn't turn off our brains. The American dream was beautiful, but it was still a dream. Liberty and justice had not yet arrived for all.

But life for many, for the growing middle class, had never been better. The world was suddenly full of mechanical wonders. When Dad and Uncle

No Bigger than a Dime

Bob listened to the Buck Rogers radio show in the 1930s, I doubt either of them thought Buck's hair-raising space adventures would ever come true. And what happened thirty years later? Astronaut Alan Shepard rode a rocket "where no man had boldly gone before!"[3] Vermonters, used to hard times long before the Great Depression arrived, blinked in surprise at the flood of goods and gadgets they could buy in stores and from mail-order houses like Sears or "Monkey" (Montgomery) Wards. For generations they had been "using it up, wearing it out, making it do, or going without." Overnight, Detroit's wartime assembly lines replaced tanks and bombers with sleek Ford and Chevy cars. Their tail fins said speed! The plug-in refrigerator pushed aside the kitchen ice-box, and Gram and Gramp could have a dish of store-bought ice cream after supper. Oh, the waistline! The washing machine and the vacuum cleaner arrived. What a godsend for Gram and Mom!

Our mahogany veneer television set had one large knob for volume and another for channels, but simple as it was, we must have felt like Stone Age hunters agog at trade axes and beads when we saw it arrive. In 1960 Chubby Checkers did the twist on American Bandstand, but right there in our living room! Margaret, the older

---
[3] From the title sequence of the 1960s television series, *Star Trek*.

sister of my best friend, Dick Watson, had already watched Elvis Presley shake his hips on the Ed Sullivan Show in '56. Rock 'n roll had reached Taftsville! Our older brother Scott combed his hair with Vitalis, went to junior high '87 Club dances at the Rec (recreation center), and set out on his first romantic quests. I still remember some of the 45 r.p.m. records he played in his bedroom, especially the doo-wop hit by the Tokens which began with these lyrics: "Hush, my darling, don't fear my darling, the lion sleeps tonight...."

Yes, we held out our hands for the manna from heaven. Gram and Gramp were still burning wood, but we weren't. Instead of feeding a cast-iron cookstove every couple hours with wood "drug" in by the wagonload, cords of wood cut by Gramp, split by "June" (a.k.a. Scott Junior, our dad) and stacked by us boys in the dog days of summer—whew!—instead of that, when the mercury dropped, we could listen for the telltale rumble of the new, thermostatically-operated oil furnace in the cellar and then warm ourselves over hot air registers. We could open a can of Campbell's chicken soup and heat it on an electric stove or eat a tomato shipped from California in January. Heck, we even had T.V. dinners and T.V. dinner trays to eat them on while we watched T.V. All this canned, packaged, processed food could be bought in one of the new grocery stores so big it was called a *super*market. People didn't have to eat beans and brined meats and roots all winter long!

With so many labor-saving devices, sometimes Gram could put her feet up and watch *As the World Turns* on the box that would later become known as the boob tube. Gramp could kick back in his recliner and watch Red Sox baseball. Leisure time! Who ever heard of such a thing? There is no doubt that much of this progress made life better for ordinary folk—especially the tetanus shot and the polio vaccine—but there were also costs. One was the loss of the old Vermont embodied in elders like Elmer Bumps and Gram and Gramp. When I talked to Duncan about this time, he was reminded of an apt passage from Dad's memoir, *Goodbye Highland Yankee*:

> In the 1920s, a watchful eye might have noticed that the self-sufficient ways that sustained the towns and farms of eastern Vermont and the border country wavered slightly and faded just a little. Then they steadied to linger on through the thirties and forties, stuck in place, like a butterfly on a mounting board, by the needle of the Great Depression. For this brief span, regional life retained the incandescence of a well-burning coal fire just before its ashes are stirred with a poker, upon which the glowing mass of red dulls and

begins to fall to pieces. For us, though we did not know it, the breakup was coming. After the war the old life, much of it rooted in medieval times, withered away along with the railroads.

When I think of the disappearance of the old Vermont, I remember the story of Romaine Tenney. He lived for sixty-four years on the small farm in Weathersfield where he had been born. He milked his twenty-odd cows by hand, hayed with horses, and lived without "the electric." After sheriff's deputies served papers to confiscate his farm and pave the way for Interstate 91, he set the barn on fire, stepped into the house, nailed the door shut, and went to meet his maker. Writer Howard Mansfield said, "Tenney was known as a quiet, friendly, jovial man. His independent, yesteryear approach made him beloved by all."

Romaine's death was tragic and poignant. It evokes, for me, that "coming to pieces" Dad talked about, and it highlights the way the interstates reached into the heart of Vermont and gave its old ticker a jolt. Luckily, the old folks and the old ways rarely ended in a fiery blaze. The inheritors of our horse-drawn farming tradition passed without much fuss as was their wont. I'm glad my brothers and I knew some of them before they slipped out the back door and walked into the beyond.

Romaine Tenney, 1900-1964 (courtesy of the Weathersfield Historical Society, Weathersfield, Vermont)

Romaine's horsepower was the old time kind (courtesy of the Weathersfield Historical Society, Weathersfield, Vermont)

We spent so much time with them and around them, their ways couldn't help but rub off on us.

Duncan told me recently about "Ghost House," a poem by Robert Frost. Its sad beauty haunts me now every time I read it in this excerpt:

> I dwell in a lonely house now
> That vanished many a summer ago,
> And left no trace but cellar walls
> And a cellar where the daylight falls
> And the purple-stemmed wild raspberries grow....
> I dwell with a strangely aching heart
> In that vanished abode there far apart
> On that disused and forgotten road
> That has no dust-bath now for the toad.
> Night comes; the black bats tumble and dart...
> It is under the small, dim summer star.
> I know not who these mute folk are
> Who share the unlit space with me—
> Those stones out under the low-limbed tree
> Doubtless bear names that the mosses mar...
> They are tireless folk, slow and sad—
> Though two close-keeping are lass and lad—
> With none of them that ever sings,
> And yet, in view of how many things,
> As sweet companions as might be had.

Frost's poetry often carries a burden of sadness, probably because he often carried that burden in his own life, so I'm glad he put "sweet companions" in the poem. Some of the "ghost people" I remember from my childhood in Happy Valley were crusty old coots and stern old biddies, but many were sweet companions. All of them had a way about them that ran marrow-deep, a way I can describe only clumsily. It was stitched from many threads, from quiet courage, vitality and dignity, a nature born of nature, born from a life spent with wind and sun, flowers and trees, animals of the forests and the fields, wild and tame. Many of them were quicker to smile than frown, and so better able to bend than break.

We saw this old farm-world spirit in Elmer Bumps' weather-creased face and twinkling eyes. We heard it in his son "Bumpy's" low, gentle voice and easy chuckle. We got a whiff of it when Si Osmer came within ten feet of us. We could hear it singing in the air when bearded Vilas Bridge walked up Happy Valley Road in the middle of a summer night, playing his carry-around radio after visiting the Cowdreys in Skunk Hollow, which was miles and miles away on foot. We could divine it in Smack Watson's "steel" as he shuffled arthritically, canes in hand, to the John Deere tractor that would take him up on the hill to bale hay. We could see it in our own grandfather, who handled a team of horses like a man when he was only fourteen and pulled logs out of the woods for a lumber company on the Connecticut River.

Some of Gramp's favored stories, ones he repeated over the years, were about horses. He had a knack with the beasts early on, and I think it was a source of real pride. All his life, he treasured those memories, and when we were young, and he was in his fifties, he had a few more chances to work with a team. Elmer still had draft horses when we moved to Happy Valley. Duncan remembers that Gramp borrowed Danny and Mike one spring to plow the garden. My younger brother must have been over the moon when he was allowed to sit atop one of those old boys as they plodded down the furrows with Gramp holding the reins. Duncan was so small his legs stuck straight out on either side of the horse's broad back. Those big fellas weighed a ton. Holy crow! Elmer thought so the day one of them stepped on his foot. I was working in the barn that night. He hurt for weeks. He had a cast, and his son Bumpy came down to help with chores, but not for long. Elmer wasn't one to lie abed.

He kept Danny and Mike around long after they were done pulling. Elmer was a holdout in that respect. The day of the draft horse had passed. Tractors plowed the furrows and hayed the fields in the '50s. Most of the horses around town ended up in Si Osmer's boneyard up on the pig farm. Their ghosts wandered the roads and turned a wary eye on cars racing by. Boys our age found buggies and sleighs dry-rotting in carriage sheds everywhere.

And that was our world. Across the valley was Si Osmer, the pig farmer and knacker who could skin a dead cow or horse or any darned animal with a saleable hide quicker than you could blink. He and his spry old mother lived side by side with a bone pile taller than their falling-down farmhouse, and had never left the 1700s where they still lived in their heads. Up the hill, kindly Elmer Bumps and his wife Mildred tended their small herd of Jersey cows, eked out a living from ever-dwindling milk checks, and sat on their small porch playing a 78 r.p.m. recording of "Peg o' My Heart" on a summer evening, a song they had first heard more than forty years earlier when they were just kids.

Across the way, at the end of the path through the hayfield, were Gramp and Gram, the millhand and the teacher, born at the turn of the century, living on a farm that had been in the Harvey family for two-hundred years but was sold when the barn burned and Ray Harvey had a heart attack. Gramp and Gram were in their fifties, and I think Gramp must have been looking for a piece of his past when they moved to Happy Valley. I think he must have persuaded Grammy that it was time to leave her Italian sisters in their West Lebanon neighborhood and buy that old farm where he and the rest of us could milk a few cows, raise chickens, grow vegetables, and cut our own wood the way so many people did when he was a kid. We never had but one cow, May, and her not for long, but we did raise chickens and harvest plenty of vegetables. I think Gramp *did* find what he was looking for there in Happy Valley, at least for a time.

Our little house was in the middle of it all. The skirl of Dad's pipes echoed in the valley on summer afternoons, and the churring of Gramp's Jeep reached us from across the field as he drove up past the sugarhouse to the woodlot. Spike barked excitedly as he chased us around the house at dusk for our last game of hide-and-seek. Mom rang the old school bell to tell us it was dinner time.

We smelled fresh-cut hay and Grammy's peonies in the summer, fermenting apples and newly-sawn maple and beech firewood in the fall, woodsmoke and wet wool in the winter, and bubbling maple syrup, pan-fried brook trout, and lilacs in the spring.

As little tykes, we boys first ventured out from our Cape Codder home in toddling steps, but soon we made longer and longer strides. Yes, Happy Valley may have been only the size of an Eisenhower dime when we were born, but it *was* our whole world. Then, we grew and grew, and the wide, wide world shrunk, and shrunk some more because Neil Armstrong walked on the moon and jets circled the globe, and soon there were no places to explore except those we imagined, especially those places of memory which were always waiting, but which were disappearing year by year under layers of time. So, let's visit those memories and say hello to the ghosts of horses, and people long gone. Let's go back to Happy Valley, for you know, life can turn on an Eisenhower dime, and we may never have another chance.

Are Alec, Duncan, and Scott uncertain about trick-or-treating, or is the sun too bright?

CHAPTER 2

Dad, Our Sean Connery

I should tell you right away *why* I saw Dad as our Sean Connery. It was because of Dad's Aunt Annie. She was one of Grammy's sisters, and we visited her often in West Lebanon, New Hampshire where Dad grew up. I enjoyed those visits because West Leb, as Dad called it, was only twenty minutes away, and I hardly had time to get carsick. I also enjoyed them because Great Aunt Annie always supplied us with generous helpings of ice cream and cookies, and because Grammy and Aunt Annie sometimes talked in an exotic language called Italian, but also because Aunt Annie was as grandmotherly as Gram and doted on her grand nephews.

She would hug us and laugh and be oh-so bubbly and fun. One of her favorite conversational gambits was to compare us to movie stars. Duncan, according to her, was the spitting image of Jimmy Dean. This was not James Dean of *Rebel Without a Cause.* This was Jimmy Dean, Fess Parker's sidekick in the early episodes of the *Daniel Boone* television series, the country western star who sang the number one hit "Big Bad John," and the owner of the Jimmy Dean Pork Sausage Company. I *loved* hearing "Big Bad John" on the radio in 1961 when I was ten years old. It was a song about a brave, "giant of a man" who died saving others in a mining tunnel cave-in. Duncan thought Aunt Annie picked Jimmy Dean as his double because he and Jimmy both had ears that stuck out, but I think she saw in her nephew another star in the making.

A young Sean Connery (disguised with glasses).
I wonder if that was Gramp's Jeep.

Dad, Our Sean Connery

Scott and I were also movie star doubles. One of us might have been Troy Donahue or Tab Hunter, but I'm not completely sure which actors were lucky enough to look like us. I think Aunt Annie "had a thing" for young, handsome, blonde actors, and any number were on the tip of her tongue when it came time to designate our doppelgangers. But she didn't limit her compliments to us young scamps. She compared Gramp to Clark Gable. Gramp might actually have passed for Gable's Rhett Butler, that iconic character from *Gone with the Wind* who said—as Gramp might have—"Frankly, Scarlett, I don't give a damn."

I don't remember Aunt Annie comparing Dad to a movie star, but I suspect she did when he was a boy and visited her house as a young nephew. If she didn't, I will rectify that oversight now. Maybe it's only because he was our dad, but Duncan and I thought Dad resembled Sean Connery. As the oldest brother, Scott has access to memories Duncan and I don't. He remembered Dad sporting a "flat-top" haircut, a style that required the use of an interesting toiletry product called a hairwax stick. It was only after Dad dispensed with the flat-top and the wax that his resemblance to "Bond, James Bond" emerged.

And now that you have the explanation for the title of this chapter, I'll talk about Dad who—movie star or not—was a star to his family. He was born in 1924 in the middle of the Roaring Twenties in his grandparents' house at the south end of McIndoe Falls, Vermont. The doctor used forceps, and this enabled the delivery but had the unhappy consequence of leaving Dad blind in one eye. Grammy was protective of him because of the injury. She had an early injury herself that might make her concern understandable. Her hearing was damaged when a family member—Aunt Rosa, I believe—tried to loosen some earwax using a bobby pin, not the tool of choice for operating in the vicinity of a delicate ear drum. Anyway, Dad was discouraged from playing risky sports like football, baseball, and basketball.

It was quite a surprise, then, when one of us boys found his fencing foils in the attic. I don't know if I was reading *The Three Musketeers* at the time, but I immediately imagined him as d'Artagnan and pictured him, with admiration, lunging and parrying with his springy sword. I'm sure we found it interesting that he took up fencing, a risky sport for a one-eyed athlete if there ever was one. His flirtation with foils may have occurred at New Hampshire's Keene State Teacher's College where he probably had to fulfill a physical education requirement and where he may have put aside Grammy's worries. We did find a protective face mask with Dad's foils, and maybe that allayed Grammy's fears if she knew of his swordplay. Then again, maybe it didn't.

Even though you can learn about Dad's boyhood from "the horse's mouth" if you read his memoir, *Goodbye Highland Yankee,* I will share my thoughts about him because a different slant of light illuminates new corners, and because what formed him was so crucial a part of what formed Scott and Duncan and me. When I view the past from the wrong end of my telescope, the figures there are small and far away, but I can still see them. I see Dad as a boy, but he is not roughhousing with other boys, not swinging a bat to hit a baseball, not taking any chances that could injure his good eye, and for that reason, perhaps being set apart. He certainly had friends, good friends, and he and Uncle Bob played together as youngsters, but I wonder if Grammy's understandable worries—and maybe Dad's own concern—turned him more inward than outward.

Like everyone, he had many moods and many contradictions, but I think it's fair to say that he was more introvert than extrovert. When we were boys, he rarely went to visit old friends from his boyhood or college days. I think we all went to visit Nelson Lapan once in Enfield, New Hampshire—Nelson was Dad's best friend during high school—but such visits were unusual.

When Mom went to work in Woodstock and made new friends, she began holding dinner parties. Dad knew all kinds of people when he worked at the Twin State Fruit Company as a boy. He was comfortable with farmers and laborers, but for some reason, I don't think he was always comfortable with some of Mom's new friends. When there were enough people at some of those early parties to allow Dad to "blend into the woodwork," he would sit somewhere by himself, well away from center stage, think his own thoughts, and sometimes even read a book. By the way, when you hear odd turns of phrase in this book (like "blend into the woodwork," etc.), it's a good bet that I heard them from Dad. I'm trying to use them on purpose because they were very much a signature of his, and because I think people born, like he was, when farms still dotted Vermont's hillsides often had especially colorful speech. Boy, he had "more of those funny sayings than Carter has little liver pills."

Anyway, I don't remember Dad ever becoming particularly close to Mom's friends, certainly not the early ones. He was a bit stiff in those early party years, but in time he loosened up and came to enjoy and respect some of the friends Mom made later like Jim and Shirley Billings, Joe and Ginny Christy, and Dr. Dorothy Spoerl, the minister at the Universalist Church. Perhaps Mom's ventures into beer brewing and wine making helped lubricate his social machinery, but a cocktail party atmosphere was foreign to him, perhaps because of patterns set in childhood. It also occurs to me that from 1947 until the late fifties, Mom and Dad's daily, weekly, and yearly social orbit revolved around family. For Dad, the world was Mom, his three boys, and his folks. For Mom to invite other people into this world must have been an adjustment for a guy who tended to be pretty self-contained.

Dad and his crew take a break from building their Happy Valley home (from top, Dad and sons, Scott and Alec).

On the other hand, Dad had already been inviting people into their world ahead of Mom through the door of Hastings Highland House. He had started importing Scottish goods in the mid-fifties at about the time he was finishing the upstairs bedrooms in our new Cape Cod house. He and Mom moved us—with excitement on both sides—into our new quarters, and the room we vacated downstairs became the Hastings Highland House office. In the center of that space was an imposing oak desk. On it sat a large sheet of blotting paper encased in a leather pad and a manual Remington typewriter upon which Dad, the two-fingered typist, composed hundreds of letters to customers, suppliers, and a wide array of curious people like himself who helped each other turn over rocks in the pursuit of their many esoteric interests (*esoteric* being another of the many words I learned from Dad that did not appear in ordinary conversation).

On shelves ranged around the room were many trappings of the Scottish highlander whose way of life England tried to crush after the Battle of Culloden in 1745. Bagpipes and practice chanters from R.G. Lawrie, Thomson, Peter Henderson, Bob Gillanders, Hardie, and other makers sat in their shipping boxes ready for sale. Also lining the shelves were tutoring books from Glasgow's College of Piping, kilts of various clan tartans, silver kilt pins, plaidies, and plaid brooches of silver each with a smoky, yellow cairngorm stone in the center. There was a claymore with a felt-lined brass basket at the hilt which protected the swordsman's hand in battle. There was a dirk Dad had made from an old file, and also the wooden sheath he made for it and decorated with Scottish thistles punched into the sterling silver trim. There were a few of the *sgian dubh* (skean dhu), a small knife a highlander kept in his stocking top and used to skin a stag, cut meat at the table, or for more nefarious purposes.

After Dad began advertising in *The Piping Times*, word spread and Hastings Highland House brought many new friends to our remote valley. They were a colorful bunch. Among them, I remember kindly Mac Hooper with his black, horn-rimmed glasses and amazing knowledge of hi-fidelity tape recorders, turntables, and amplifiers, all relatively new, space-age technology. In later years Duncan and I both contacted him, and I was touched when he said Dad was as nice a guy as he ever worked with.

Then, there was a moon-faced, friendly fellow I'll just call Big Dave. His arrival was always heralded by the *putt-putt-putt* of his Vespa motor scooter. He once gave me a ride on the scooter which was both thrilling and terrifying because I wasn't sure of his skill. Perhaps that was because—as Duncan reminded me—Dave suffered a self-inflicted injury in our presence. He was a Cutco knife salesman, and on one visit he convinced Mom and Dad to witness a demonstration of the amazing sharpness of a Cutco kitchen knife.

"You can slice right through a piece of paper without any tearing at all!" he said with enthusiasm. He held the paper Dad proffered, sliced quickly through it, and continued the downward motion, slicing through his pants and into the flesh of his thigh. Blood poured from the wound, and Dave—somewhat abashed—asked Mom if she had any bandages. Dad had always advised us boys that in using a knife, "one should always cut away from one's self." Dave's demonstration made the point most forcefully.

And there were many others. Doc Staples was a well-dressed, gentlemanly physician who practiced in nearby Hanover and took piping lessons from Dad. Another Upper Valley resident was the elderly, likable Maude French who was a great fan of West Lebanon's Pipers of Ben Dhu. Dad and his longtime friend Fordyce Ritchie started this marching band in the '50s, and Maude was often one of the excited bystanders who lined the street of each Upper Valley town where the band played from Memorial Day through Labor Day. As I sift my memory for more names of those who sought out Hastings Highland House and then struck up a friendship with Dad, one stands out.

What I remember first about Doc Cunliffe was that he was nearly sixty when his path crossed ours, and yet, at this advanced age, he had married a much younger second wife named Donna. If he was ancient, as I thought him to be, he was also animated and vigorous. He had seven kids, one of whom was an attractive daughter nicknamed Chee-Chee. She was about my age or Scott's, and quite—well—nubile. Doc was born in Manchester, England and moved to the United States as a boy. He had a surprisingly high voice, mischievous, twinkling eyes, and degrees in science, medicine, and theology. By the time we met him, he had helped found the College of Criminal Justice at Northeastern University, and he was—as people used to say—"well off." We visited the Cunliffe summer home in Walpole, New Hampshire a few times, and we brothers were impressed. They had a swimming pool! At that point in our young lives, such a luxury was the stuff of movies.

Once Doc took us to see the Pipes and Drums of the Scots Guards at Boston Gardens. We rode in his station wagon, and he drove fast—wicked fast! He passed cars on the left and right, weaving in and out of traffic, and I was sure the wagon was going to lift off the highway and fly at any moment. Of course, I was a bumpkin from Vermont, and I was used to Dad's sedate driving, so maybe I'm exaggerating Doc's rocketship speed, but jeez!—it felt like we were riding a lightning bolt.

Doc never became an expert piper, but he was an expert in so many other fields, it didn't matter. The man was brilliant, fascinating, and hilarious. I still remember a book he gave Mom and Dad. William Longgood's *Poisons in Your Food* was published in 1960, and the title refers to the dangerous amounts of pesticides, herbicides, and other toxic substances like strontium 90 that people were ingesting with their daily bread. Doc opened our eyes to the dangers of pollution even before Rachel Carson published *Silent Spring* in '62. And we only met Doc because Dad played the bagpipes. This was to happen over and over again in our lives. Dad's "esoteric" interests attracted people who enriched our lives and minds.

After meeting so many of his piping friends over the years, I once asked Dad how he acquired his passion for piping and all things Scottish. I wondered how a kid raised in a Yankee river town like West Lebanon, New Hampshire could be more than marginally aware of bagpipes and Scotland. He said he heard the Black Watch regimental pipe band on a Canadian radio station when he was young, and that captured his imagination. Growing up in the thirties, of course, the

Doctor Frederick Cunliffe (courtesy of Northeastern University Library, Boston, Massachusetts).

---

radio was for him what television was for us in the '50s. It was an entirely novel, magical box. He described with great affection favorite radio dramas like *Jack Armstrong, the All-American Boy*, *The Shadow* (with 22-year-old Orson Welles as the voice of Lamont Cranston), *The Green Hornet*, *The Lone Ranger*, and many others. Perhaps Dad's birthplace in Caledonia County also made him fond of the Highlands early on. As its name suggests, it was founded by Scots, and Dad must have rubbed shoulders with many a man whose forbears came here with fond remembrances of the Highlands if not of the British who drove them out.

I was surprised to learn from a 1947 entry in Mom's Keene State diary that Dad once showed up at her door in a kilt. What!? He was only 23! I very much doubt his friends were wearing kilts. Dad—what a great, crazy guy. Yes, he fell in love with the Scots, and that led in a few years to his first set of pipes. I know they arrived just before Christmas in 1951 because he brought them to the hospital to show me and Mom right after I was born. Mom said he opened the box and was as proud of his pipes as she was of her new baby boy. She loved to tell that story with a little smile that nowadays might be accompanied with an eye roll, but she lived in a different time and genuinely loved his passion. Thinking of her diary again, every other entry ended with "I love, Scott" or "I love Scott so much." She was smitten. Anyway, the pipes and the Scots did become a lifelong passion for Dad, and if you need more proof, think of his sons' names: Scott, Alec, and Duncan. Aye, I'll admit that Scott was named after Dad, but they're Scottish names all three, nevertheless.

He began learning the pipes using a practice chanter and the *College of Piping Tutor*. Once he finished building our house, he advertised in *The Valley News* for anyone interested in forming a bagpipe band. Dick Durrell, Art Forten, Doc Mcleod, Sheldon Bellimer, and George Fordyce Ritchie among others answered the call. That band of merry men became the aforementioned Pipers of Ben Dhu. Ritchie, as he was

Mom and Dad… "I love you so much."

known, became Dad's piping mentor and his lifelong friend. Mom, always handy with a sewing machine, made kilts for the bandsmen, and we often traveled in our Chevrolet Fleetline sedan with its roomy bench seats and no safety belts to hear the band play in towns nearby.

I still remember the festive mood of the people crowding the sidewalks on a warm Fourth of July day. The band would appear down the street, their shoes hitting the tarmac in unison as they marched toward us. Drum Major Doc Mcleod led the way, majestically swinging his five-foot mace and looking even taller than usual in his bearskin hat. Dick Durrell alternately twirled one felt-covered mallet and hit the big bass drum with the other one, booming out a cadence that kept everybody marching in step. Then, at Doc's signal, each piper gave his pipe bag a punch as he blew it up, and suddenly the thrilling skirl of the pipes filled the street, and the crowd hushed as the Pipers of Ben Dhu strode by playing "Scotland the Brave."

The Pipers of Ben Dhu. Pipe Major Scott Hastings, Jr. at left. A well-turned out bunch!

Fordyce Ritchie and Tom Standeven were Dad's most memorable piping friends. Tom only visited us a few times because he came all the way from Philadelphia by train, but he was a welcome guest. He was a prize-winning Uilleann piper and was kind enough to help Dad get off to a good start on the so-called Irish elbow pipes. Tommy had an interesting way of drinking Guinness Stout, the popular Irish beer. He mixed it half and half with milk. I thought it was odd, but just the other night I drank a commercially brewed "milk stout," so maybe Tommy was ahead of his time. The *ceilidhs* (pronounced kaylees) or kitchen parties we had when Tom visited were great fun. They lasted into the wee, small hours and were full of storytelling and wonderful Irish music. Sometimes he brought friends, one of whom had been a member of the Irish Republican Army.

Ritchie was Dad's closest friend throughout his adult life. In the summer, we would hear the throaty rumble of a motorcycle, and he would roll into our driveway on his 650 BSA, one of those old British bikes that inevitably leaked oil and required frequent tinkering but was a classic ride. Always, Dad and Ritchie would play the pipes and then talk about old tunes like "The Battle of Killiecrankie" or Ritchie's latest thinking about the *piobaireachd* (peebrock), the classical music of the pipes. They might also talk about The Pipers of Ben

CAP PISTOLS, CARDBOARD SLEDS & SEVEN RUSTY NAILS

Dhu while it was still a going concern. By the time the band folded, Dad and Ritchie were well known in the Upper Valley and were often asked to play at weddings, funerals, Burns Night celebrations, and always at the annual Dartmouth College Alumni Reunion. I joined Dad and Ritchie for that reunion when I was eighteen, and I felt as if I had finally passed my "piping exam."

All those years when Dad played the pipes daily are engraved in my memory like letters cut in granite, and I'm sure they are in Scott and Duncan's memories as well. I will never forget riding my bike pell-mell down the Low Road to Taftsville on a fine summer day and returning home in time for dinner. By late afternoon, I would be tired from playing ball or beating up on Danny Lambert (this only happened once—with Dick Watson's help—and Danny deserved it because he picked on us way too much). I would get an Orange Crush soda to wet my whistle and begin the long haul up through the village and into the woods where the Low Road wandered uphill along the brook.

Memory is taking me back there now. By the time I near the open meadows of Happy Valley, I'm huffing and puffing and pushing my bike. Then, just when my spirits begin to flag, I hear faintly and from far away the sound of the pipes echoing off the hills. I throw my doldrums into the bushes and march up the road like

Dad's oldest friend, George Fordyce Ritchie, with his trusty British bike. Ritchie won a piping championship in Boston at the age of sixteen. He was, as the oldtimers might have said, some good.

a trooper, "The Road to the Isles" pushing me onward and upward, the pipes a better tonic than the Orange Crush. Dad is up there on the hill, maybe a quarter-mile away still, and on comes "Scots Wha Hae" and "Johnny Cope" and "Kantara to El Arish," and even though I don't know those are the names of the tunes at that moment, the tunes themselves land in my memory and rise to the surface again years later when I begin learning the pipes myself.

I heard Dad's pipes on many an afternoon as I rode my bike up the Low Road and into Happy Valley. Always, the sound lifted my spirits!

The story of Scotty the Piper could be a book, but he had many other sides. I go to Duncan's house now and see the furniture my brother made in his woodshop, think of the beautiful dining room table Scott crafted in his shop, think of my own lesser but no less useful skills with woodworking tools, and I know we are all grateful that Dad taught us how to use a chisel, a plane, a rule, a hammer, a saw, and all the other tools of the trade. In my living room I have a beautiful, colonial-style end table he made. I think of him in the cellar where he built our Cold War fallout shelter, and where the oil furnace rumbled on in the winter whenever the thermostat upstairs called for heat.

He set up a lathe under a bare lightbulb turned on by a hanging string. On that lathe, he turned out the drones, chanter, and blowpipe for the first set of bagpipes he made. Later, when his wide-ranging curiosity landed on muzzle-loading rifles, he bought a hardware kit from Dixie Gun Works and built a Kentucky rifle. When he was a boy, he built a couple boats, one of which he used to run the rapids where Wilder Dam was later built in 1950. Once, he took his Grandfather Oliver out in the rowboat he built as a boy of sixteen. Great Gramp quietly smoked his pipe for a while and then pointed to an iron ring in a nearby ledge.

"That's where we used to boom the logs," he said. "We'd hold them back so we could feed them through the canal locks a few at a time and avoid a jam." He was talking about working the log drives that filled the river every spring when the ice went out. I wondered if a circle was being completed there. Although little was ever mentioned about Great Gramp Oliver's childhood, he apparently left home after his mother died. The story goes that at the age of ten he was farmed out to an old couple who used him hard. He ran away and was taken in by the Shakers in Enfield, New Hampshire. The Shakers were master woodworkers, and I believe I heard that Great Gramp Oliver apprenticed to them and acquired some of those skills himself. Does that explain Dad's early interest in woodworking? Was that interest awakened by his grandfather when Dad visited the farm in McIndoes? Probably we will never know, but it seems plausible to me.

What else do I say about Dad? You may know about the books he wrote, but you may not know about the one never published. It was a children's story titled The Adventures of Pipe Major Sam Scott, and it begins like this: "Once upon a time—it wasn't your time or my time, but it was somebody's time long ago—a weaver wanting power to turn the works of his mill built a great dam of cut stone just where the Ottauquechee River drops with a fearsome crash into the mists and swirling winds of the Maw of the Gorge."

Suddenly, with these words, I hear him again. He is reading to us from the first chapter of *The Wind in the Willows*. Mole has burst into the sunshine, and after his long winter nap he skips with glee across the greening meadow. Coming to the riverbank, he meets his old friend, Rat. Dad reads so well I see the characters before me cavorting in the warmth of a spring day. I am carried along by the tale until my bed becomes a boat softly rocking on the surface of the river. My eyelids lower and rise and lower again, and I drift downstream toward sleep. At just the right time, Dad closes the book and turns out the light.

Dad, Our Sean Connery

And I am nearing that time in this chapter. I don't want to put you to sleep, so I will draw to a close with a few more anecdotes about Dad that appear on the silver screen in my mind when I turn on my rattling, old reel-to-reel projector of remembrances. You may find it peculiar that I remember this one, but what can I say—memory is erratic and has a mind of its own. One summer day we were in our Cape Cod house in Happy Valley and Dad had his shirt off. By that time, he was probably in his late thirties, a hairy-chested, full-grown man. Maybe that was why the following carnival trick seemed so hilarious. "Watch this, boys," he said. He bent over slightly, placed his hands on his knees, sucked in an enormous breath, and suddenly his stomach collapsed on either side of a hard ridge of abdominal muscles that ran from the lower sternum to his belly button and disappeared below his belt. We burst out laughing with delight. We tend to think that profound events or words make the most lasting impression, so I don't know why this one stuck with me. I suppose it is explained by my own, sometimes peculiar character.

Another moment with Dad also sticks in my mind, and again I don't know why. When we were wee lads, we played first on the sandbank next to the house with toy trucks and steam shovels (see cover photo). Dad eventually set up targets on that sandbank and taught us how to shoot the Remington 0.22 caliber rifles he gave us. These were the rifles he used to hunt squirrels on Craft Hill in West Leb. As time passed, we moved farther and farther away from that sandbank and our yard. We finally got permission to play across the fence in the old brickyard where there was a pint-sized frog pond. Those poor frogs. We made them captains of their own little boats (floating sticks) and launched them on voyages from port to port around the edge of the eight-foot diameter pond. Clearly, they never embraced the captain's code of conduct because they abandoned ship at every opportunity.

Beyond the frog pond and Elmer's pasture was a forest of small pines we called The Little Woods. Playing there was a big step. When we entered that unknown territory, our home-sweet-home disappeared from view as the pine branches closed behind us. Mother Machree! What if we got lost? After several explorations we got familiar with the lay of the land, and such worries were forgotten. One of the entertaining spots in The Little Woods was the Elephant Tree. A long branch with an upturned limb at the end reached out horizontally from a stout, ancient maple tree. If we leaped and caught hold of it or boosted each other up, we could scramble onto the branch, scootch out to the upturned limb at the end and bounce slowly up and down like Tarzan when Tantor the elephant allowed him to sit on his upturned trunk and carried him wherever the ape-man wanted to go.

Sometimes we accompanied Dad on forays into the woods or fields. One spring ritual was checking the condition of the spring. Our water supply consisted of two wooden barrels sunk into a wet spot a couple hundred yards above our house. Watching carefully, we learned, with some horror, the purpose behind this annual visit. Dad would pull the large wooden cover off the barrels and peer down into the clear spring water. Sometimes, the water didn't have the desired clarity. This was usually because the body of a drowned mouse was floating on the surface and separating into tufts of fur and soggy bits. Dad would scoop out the mouse remains with a homemade cheesecloth net, and then pour a jug of Clorox into the well. We would have to get drinking water from Gram and Gramp until we ran enough water through the pipes to make the water potable again.

On one foray into the woods, Dad accompanied me. I'm not sure if this was at my request or if Dad recognized that I was at a tipping point and might need some guidance. There have been a number of such points in my life, and Dad was an invaluable guide at such times. This particular time was not fraught with danger, I suppose. Still, it loomed large in my imagination. We walked into The Little Woods and made our way uphill until we reached its upper boundary. Ahead, taller pines, much taller pines, clustered together more closely than the pines in The Little Woods. A path into the darkness under the trees lay before us. Dad looked at me, and then continued confidently on, following the path. We walked for a long time, and—more woods-wise by that age—I kept my eyes open for landmarks I would recognize the next time I was there. Later, quite some time later, we emerged from The Big Woods at the far upper corner of the hayfields above our house. I had never ventured that far. Dad stepped on the lower strand of a barbed wire fence and raised the upper one. I squeezed through, and then he climbed over. We stood looking down on the peaceful scene below, on home, on the stream that ran down through the middle of the neatly mown fields, and I had the sense of having experienced something special, of having learned something. I realized later I was learning how to stay on my path when the way looked dark and I was scared. Mom and Dad both said to me more than once, "Alec, you're going to have to learn the hard way." They weren't entirely wrong. Some of us just do, I guess. But many a time when I've had a fear to face, when I've chosen to learn something the hard way, I've remembered that moment at the edge of The Big Woods, remembered his hand taking mine, and I've done what I needed to do, grateful that he showed me the way.

*Scott Edison Hastings, Junior, 1924-1990.
In later years he was still as handsome as Sean.*

CHAPTER 3

Mom, Woman of Mystery

This week, brother Scott asked for stories about Mom. I've been thinking about her the last couple nights, especially after throwing a log on the fire at one a.m. and lying awake in bed afterward. What a challenge it is to remember the past! First, there is the Rashomon effect (seeing the past through the lens of our own experience), and then there is the hole-in-the-bucket problem.

Here is how I picture memory. We drop a bucket down a well and bring it up full of water. It's full, at least, if our memory is crystal clear. More than likely, it is not full because—unless we have a photographic memory like Teddy Roosevelt or Nikola Tesla—we can't remember every detail. In that case, we discover a hole in the bucket. Some of our memories have leaked out. If we have an exceptionally good memory, the hole is near the rim of the bucket, and only a few of our recollections have dribbled away. If we have a poor memory, the hole is near the bottom, and we are left with only a few tablespoons of memory.

Memories are surprisingly slippery, and age is not the only factor that affects memory. A single, traumatic event (like my spinal tap at the age of four), for instance, can leave a lasting impression while an event that has become routine (like the time I stepped on rusty nail number seven) may be forgotten even though it, too, made quite an impression at the time. It is also apparently true that we remember our adolescence and early adulthood more vividly than other times in our lives. Researchers call it the "renaissance bump," and speculate that the reason for it has to do with our brains being brand new and with our experience of many "firsts" at this time of life.

As I raise Mom from the well of memory, I see that the hole in my bucket is near the middle. The hole is closer to the rim when I raise Dad and Gramp. It doesn't take a brain surgeon to understand this. Memories of Dad and Gramp stick because we boys looked up to them and wanted to be like them. We were intrigued with hammers, logging chains, chainsaws, guns, bagpipes, with the stuff of the man's world that awaited us. I still remember being instructed by Dad in the proper use of a hammer when I was actually allowed up on the roof of the new barn he and Gramp were building. Whoa! Exciting!

Men were always nearby doing something we

found interesting. A bulldozer operator—perhaps our neighbor Bumpy—graded a site for our new house and left a bank of sand exposed at the end of the driveway. Soon, Dad began laying cement blocks for the foundation of our new house. When we tired of watching him, we scooped out holes in the sand bank with our own bulldozers and hauled the sand away in toy dump trucks. Years later, we set up targets on that sand bank when Dad taught us how to shoot a rifle. But before the gun came the knife. Dad demonstrated the "cut *away* from yourself" technique, and when Scott was finally entrusted with a jackknife, one of his first experiences with a blade was carving a jack o' lantern. That also gave him practice in being brave because he had to get stitches when he sliced into his hand. Yes, these and many other activities were rites of initiation. I think we were less fascinated with learning to wash the dishes.

And "there's the rub" as Dad and the Bard would say. Mom and Gram did all the women's work, and learning to vacuum the living room or make my bed did not appeal to me as much as watching Gramp tie a trucker's hitch or making a bread board in the Hartford Junior High woodshop while Dad lined up a Monday morning project for his students. Like as not, while tying down a load of furniture, Gramp would tell about a tarp-covered truckload of bootleg booze coming into the mill yard in East Ryegate one night during Prohibition. Or while I was sanding a breadboard in the shop, Dad might talk about cutting cordwood with Nelson Lapan when they were in high school. My first dip into Mom and Gram's bucket doesn't bring up many such stories. Either my dipper has a hole too, or doing the dishes didn't inspire Mom to tell stories. She was probably too busy checking

Mom (at right) with other Keene State students harvesting potatoes during or shortly after World War II.

for food still stuck to the plates we had washed to be telling stories.

Then again, maybe with the hole in my bucket, I just don't remember the stories she did tell. I do know this—I appreciate the selflessness she showed in doing a thousand-and-one menial jobs every week that went unnoticed. She was the unsung heroine of our household who kept the fires of family contentment burning. Recently, I read the diary she kept after Dad passed away, and this excerpt saddened me: "The last few days have been full of the realization that I have no direction." I know, from the way I felt after my wife Debbie passed away, that there was probably more than one reason for this lack of direction, but I think a life given over so much to her family was one reason she found herself suddenly adrift. Even after she did the remaining work for the publication of Dad's last book, *Up in the Morning Early*, her diary reflects her selflessness: "I hope it goes well as it will be wonderful for Scott to have another book to his credit."

If I can't come up with many stories about Mom, I can at least try to paint her portrait. Like a lot of kids, I was always curious to know what my parents were like when they were young, so let's start with her background. What I can piece together from conversations I had with Dad and Uncle Pete, is that the Richards' childhood sometimes smacked of Old Mother Hubbard and her bare cupboard. Yes, times were occasionally hard and the larder almost empty. Of course, that was true for a good many families during the Great Depression and World War II. Depression anecdotes about scarcity were always looming in the background when we were growing up. "Waste not, want not" was a pithy saying oft repeated. I believe Mom once shared the menu for a Richards' supper: potatoes. I'm not sure how often that meal rotated through the menu. Let's hope it was only once or twice during a lean time in winter.

I do think I heard that the Richards grew vegetables, so hopefully the fat times of summer brought peas, beans, corn, and tomatoes to the table. Mom was born in 1927, the same year Gramp William Richards started working as a millhand for the Brown Paper Company in Berlin, New Hampshire. He stayed until '38, which means the family was in that sulfur-reeking town for the entire Great Depression. We were told that Gramp Richards admired Eugene Debs, the Socialist Party leader who ran for President from his prison cell in 1920 and was a nominee for the Nobel Peace Prize in '24. Gramp must have voted for Franklin Delano Roosevelt in '32. As President, FDR initiated new, perhaps Debs-inspired, social programs that created a "safety net" for the poor and the working class. It was about time. One of the few stories I remember from Mom's side of the family was about a mill worker who fell in a vat of the sulfuric acid they used to turn pulpwood into paper pulp. All that was left of him were the brass buttons from his overalls. It was the same mill that employed Gramp Richards.

Elsie Elizabeth Richards in Berlin, New Hampshire. What a cutie!

After Berlin, the family moved to a series of other small New Hampshire towns: Nottingham, Exeter, Hudson, and Goffstown. They moved a lot. In fact, Mom told Duncan she went to thirteen different schools. I believe she earned a varsity letter in basketball at Goffstown, a fact I put in my plus column for Mom because I played high school basketball as well. It was so much like her to never make much of the fact that *she* played ball. I think she might have graduated from Goffstown. From there, the family moved to Leominster,

Mom's father, William Richman Richards, 1903-1952. She suffered a great loss when he died at 49. This is the one picture of him I remember seeing in our house when I was a kid. Classic north country attire!

Massachusetts, then to Plainfield and Charlestown, New Hampshire. They finally returned to Exeter where Gramp Richards died in 1952 after a series of heart attacks.

According to Dad, Mom adored her father. He died young, at the age of 49, a year after I was born. Mom was devastated. Dad respected his father-in-law and described him as a well-read man with a sharp intellect. After the mill, his steadiest employment was as an executive of Boy Scout Councils in southern New Hampshire. I don't suppose the Boy Scouts paid especially well, but that work might have suited him given the accident he suffered after enlisting with the U.S. Army in 1923. He was belowdecks on a troop ship when—according to Uncle Pete—a man dropped a wrench on Gramp's head from a catwalk above. He suffered a serious concussion and convalesced for months in a San Francisco hospital before being released and discharged from the service. I never understood exactly how the injury handicapped him afterward, whether he suffered headaches or depression or impairment to his thinking, but Uncle Pete said it did hamper his ability to work. This must have meant that Uncle Bill and Mom, the two oldest kids, had to grow up a little faster and work a little harder than normal to help provide for Uncle Bud, Aunt Bev, Uncle Bruce, and Uncle Pete. When I think about Mom's childhood, I feel I understand her better now than I did as a young man.

And much of what I remember about the Mom I knew as a boy must have carried over from her own childhood. She worked her fingers to the nub caring for her family. She kept a neat, clean house. Scott remembers this because he, like Dunc and me, didn't enjoy being roused from his Saturday morning slumbers by the annoying sound of Mom running the vacuum cleaner. Of course, Mom quickly silenced our complaints by assigning vacuuming duties to us. She kept a spic-and-span kitchen, and we had our jobs there too, setting the table, clearing the table, washing the dishes, drying the dishes, and sweeping the floor. How we bickered sometimes about whose turn it was. No wonder she switched us across the backs of our legs with a flyswatter when she'd had enough!

When we acted up, Mom wasn't apt to say, "You wait until your father gets home." She was perfectly capable of dealing with us herself. As Dorothy Richards' daughter, she probably had plenty of chances to see discipline swiftly and effectively administered. Our own experience as Gram Richards' grandsons taught us that she would brook no nonsense. Duncan and I researched our Richards' ancestors and discovered that they came to the New Hampshire seacoast in the

Mom, Woman of Mystery

1600s along with a host of other Puritans, a Protestant sect that heartily endorsed the biblical adage, "Spare the rod and spoil the child." I imagine if Mom and her siblings got out of line, they got the switch across the backs of *their* legs. Mom's flyswatter was a modern variant on that time-honored implement of persuasion, but it was not her only lever of enforcement.

Duncan reminded me of the day he said, "Shit!" That is not a word appreciated by New England women of Puritan descent. Mom warned him that if he ever said that word again, she would wash his mouth out with soap. He immediately repeated himself: "Shit!" She marched him into the bathroom, took up a bar of Ivory soap, and sanitized his mouth and speech.

While on the subject of discipline, I suppose I should mention "the belt." In the 1950s and '60s, corporal punishment was still considered a perfectly legitimate way to convince children of the error of their ways. For serious trespasses, Dad would turn us over his knee, double up his belt and give us a few good whacks on our bums. It had to be pretty serious for him to do this, and I don't think his heart was really in it because I don't remember it happening more than a few times. To take away some of the sting, one of us tried padding himself with a comic book to ward off the worst of the blows. Of course, Dad wasn't fooled, and he waited patiently while his son sheepishly removed an old copy of *Superman* from the seat of his pants. I wonder what Dad thought. No doubt, he smiled to himself and then felt even worse about performing his duty. Maybe he and Mom decided the belt was too much because eventually they switched to one of Mom's hairbrushes. I still remember that pale blue, plastic brush. Fortunately, they used the back side of the brush, not the side with the bristles. But still—ouch!

Most of the time they disciplined us by giving us extra chores or by sending us to our rooms, sometimes without supper, but even then, they usually relented and showed up with something to eat after everyone else had left the table. Mom loved us with all her heart, but I think at times in her life, she wasn't quite sure how to deal with us. I'm sure she had heard another biblical adage as a child: "Obey thy parents." When that and a switch to our fannies didn't always yield the desired result, I imagine she became discouraged and irritated. I remember a poem she recited for me, sometimes in an almost pleading tone: "There was a little girl who had a little curl right in the middle of her forehead, and when she was good, she was very, very good, and when she was bad, she was horrid." Mom wanted me to take the hint and not be horrid. The only thing I took from Longfellow's poem was offense at being compared to a girl. Sigh. Raising three boys must have been hard. But in the end, her long-suffering patience was rewarded. Her granddaughters Asia, Maria, Josey, Chelsea, and Calley were a great blessing in her later years.

Speaking of going to bed without supper brings to mind another of Mom's jobs—feeding time at the zoo. She put three squares on the table every day. Breakfast wasn't hard. Basically, it meant pouring Sugar Pops or Rice Krispies or Cheerios into a bowl and adding milk. My brothers and I actually learned to do this for ourselves before too many years passed. She could depend on some peace and quiet at the breakfast table because we usually became engrossed in reading the cereal boxes, which offered "free" soldiers or dinosaurs or other toys if we sent in enough box tops. Lunch was often tuna fish, peanut butter and jelly, or peanut butter and marshmallow sandwiches with Campbell's chicken with rice or tomato soup from a can. Supper, however, meant Mom actually cooked.

As I remember this, my spirit droops a little even today because—honestly—she wasn't a great cook. Yeah, I was probably a finicky eater, but man, those mashed potatoes were a lumpy, gray glop. And salmon pea wiggle and chipped beef on toast? Ugh! In her defense I ate a lot of similar Yankee cooking at my friends' houses. It wasn't what you'd call *haute cuisine*. If you had meat, potatoes, and a vegetable on your plate, you were to consider yourself lucky. More than once we were admonished to "think of the starving kids in China!" Also frequently heard was this order: "You can't leave the table until you clean your plate." I used to jam mashed potatoes and peas on the underside of the table—until I got caught. Then, I tried putting food in my napkin and asking to be excused to the bathroom where I flushed it down the toilet. Sometimes Spike, our beagle-German shepherd cross was my more-than-willing accomplice in furtive food disposal. One night, I sat at the table for an hour after dinner was over. A whole hour. I pushed food around listlessly with my fork—"Don't play with your food!"—as shadows lengthened and day eventually turned to night. It was an eternity. I don't remember who won the battle of wills. If I did, it was a pyrrhic victory because the battle was surely joined again the next night. No wonder Mom breathed a sigh of relief when we went to bed. No wonder I did. I should mention that Mom's cooking improved in later years when she was no longer strapped to the endlessly turning wheel of daily duties. I remember, for example, that she learned to make a fine beef bourguignon. She served it with pride to her guests and even to her grown-up sons on occasion. I didn't wrap any of it in a napkin either.

Mom, Woman of Mystery

I should make special mention in this brief and incomplete inventory of Mom's duties of one of the most difficult: keeping us safe. I'm sure that was no easy task. From the time I started head-banging in my crib, she knew I was going to be trouble. I was two, and we were still living at Gram and Gramps' when, left briefly to my own devices on the back lawn, I discovered a rusty, open can of tar. It was a hot summer day, and the tar was most interestingly gooey. By the time Mom discovered me, I had daubed it on my clothes, hair and face. Oh boy. I think kerosene was used in the cleanup. When we moved to our new house across the field, we were told daily to "go out and play." There was a hemlock tree about twenty yards from the house, and a shelf of ledge stuck out of the ground underneath it. We were forbidden to climb this tree because of the possibility that we would fall and break our necks on that ledge. We, of course, climbed it every chance we got and took our spankings when we got caught.

If Mom had only known how hard we were to kill, she probably would have slept better at night. Once Scott and I were facing each other on the two bench seats in the back of Gramp's Jeep. Gramp was driving up Sugar Hill to Elmer's farm at a pretty good clip. It was September, and we were eating apples. We hit a bump, and I looked up just in time to see Scott tumbling

Mom (née Elsie Elizabeth Richards, 1927-2002) with her boys on July 5, 1991, a year and two days after Dad passed away. From left, Duncan, Scott, and Alec.

over the side. He fell out! Gramp stopped, Scott ran up to us, climbed back in, and on up to Elmer's we went. If I know Gramp, he said, "Don't tell your mother." Eventually, I think Mom realized it was impossible to keep us entirely safe, or maybe we just got old enough that she crossed her fingers and hoped for the best. By that time her instructions were simpler: "Come back when you hear the dinner bell."

But on to a few of Mom's other jobs, or I'll spend the entire chapter about Mom reciting the trespasses of her sons. She also kept us in clean clothes, mended them when holes appeared in the knees of our blue jeans, and outfitted us with our Sunday best. Sunday attire was

A Sunday-best picture taken before sports coats were required. At a guess, I would say those ties are clip-ons. Duncan and I look way too happy to be going to church. Scott's expression is more appropriate to the occasion.

another sore point for me. I'm sorry, but I just hated those little blazers with the too-short sleeves, the highwater pants, and those darn loafers. I don't know why, but I positively despised loafers and saw no reason why I couldn't wear my black-and-white Converse sneakers to church if the Universalists were so doggone progressive.

Nope, no dice, because we were going to church, like it or not, and we were going in our best clothes. If you want a portrait of Mom, this is an area where she stands out in stark contrast to her Hastings in-laws—or maybe I should say outlaws. The Hastings were not big on churchgoing. Mom was. She went to church "religiously." I mean, every Sunday! When we were young, Dad would go on Christmas and Easter, but Sundays were a good time for him to catch up on Hastings Highland House business and on his million-and-one other endeavors. And truthfully, Dad did not seem entranced by hymn singing, bible reading, and after-church socializing. I don't think I *ever* saw Gramp in a church. Maybe he went when a close relative died, but not otherwise. Grammy apparently used to go to church in West Lebanon, but she gave it up when she moved to Happy Valley.

But Mom? She loved it! I don't know if she was a true believer. She didn't give us a lot of religious instruction, so I'm skeptical of this idea. Maybe she figured we would get that in Sunday school from Ed Hawkes while we were putting pictures of Jesus and Mary in coloring books and eating dollops of paste which actually tasted better than Mom's potatoes. As I ponder Mom's motives now, a light comes on. Mom wanted to get out of the house! She loved being able to visit with other grownups before and after the service. She eventually became a pillar of the church and volunteered for all bake sales, rummage sales, and any other church activity.

Mom, Woman of Mystery

Doing the math quickly, it occurs to me that she was the prisoner of three rambunctious boys day in and day out for eleven years, from 1949 to 1960, when Duncan finally—thank God!—enrolled in first grade, and the three of us were ensconced in the hallowed halls of the Woodstock Elementary School every day. Soon after that, she and Dad bought a second-hand '58 Ford Fairlane, and—blow the trumpets!—she went to work! Joe Nalibow hired her to clerk at the Woodstock Pharmacy.

I think work and church were two really significant parts of Mom's life that I never thought about at the time, but that now seem so important to understanding her. Coming from those hard Depression and War years when the Richards were struggling to make ends meet, I think she wanted to pull herself up by her bootstraps, climb the rungs of the social ladder, and *be somebody*. I guess we all have our own definitions of what it means to be somebody. Dad's had to do with all kinds of artistic and creative projects he could pursue—by himself. Mom's had to do with being out in the world where she could do useful work and meet and be a part of her community. She did that.

Because she married Dad, she didn't complete her education at Keene State Teacher's College, so she had to do unskilled work for a while, but I don't think she ever had a moment's regret that she married Dad and left college without graduating. I just reread the diary Mom kept while she and Dad were at college in 1947. In her entry for July 19, not long before they married on August 23, she says, "We loved and talked and adored being together after that horribly long 2 weeks [apart]. He means more to me than all the world and makes all peace within me." Entry after entry in that diary ended with, "I love Scott." She surely did.

Anyway, I'm sure it didn't take long for the word to spread in Woodstock that Mom was hardworking, efficient, and smart. She left the pharmacy, and took another clerical job at the local office of the University of Vermont Extension Service. That office was in the Town Hall adjacent to the U.S. Soil Conservation Office, and the municipal offices, and there she made new friends like Jack and Jan Griggs, and Jim and Shirley Billings. Slowly but surely, she kept meeting people, making friends, and proving herself in the workplace. She passed the Vermont Real Estate Exam, and Georgina Williamson—an old acquaintance from the Universalist Church—hired her to sell properties in Woodstock. I bet she was good at it. She was the kind of person to do her homework, and people trusted her.

At the beginning of this chapter, I called Mom a woman of mystery. Mom and I didn't always see eye to eye, and we became estranged toward the end of her life. She loved me and I loved her, but I think it's fair to say we didn't always understand each other. Although the title of this chapter may sound tongue-in-cheek, Mom really was a mystery to me at times, and I'm sure I was a mystery to her. A lot of water has gone over the dam now. It's been eighteen years since she passed away. In writing this chapter, I thought a lot about her and tried once again to get a handle on who she really was.

With that in mind, I was reading her other diary, the one she wrote after Dad died. She loved Dad with all her heart and soul, and losing him was, I'm sure, the worst thing that ever happened to her. She was broken. What she wrote about her grief brought me back to 2003 and the utter sadness I felt over losing Debbie. It was certainly the worst thing that had ever happened to me. And it was a sad experience Mom and I had in common. It made my heart ache for her. In writing this chapter, in talking to my brothers about Mom, and in putting the pieces of Mom's life together in a way I never really had, I think I do understand her better than I once did. I wish both Mom and Dad had been able to know and love Deb and my wonderful stepchildren, Jake and Katie, but it wasn't to be (how I dislike putting the word "step" before children!). In the end she did her best for me, and I did my best for her, and if our best could have been better, I guess it only proves we were both imperfect humans, and I don't know of any other kind. I'll end this chapter with a poem about the childhood Scott, Duncan, and I shared, a childhood where Mom was always there, in the doorway, calling us home.

The Bell

Mickey Mouse bursts through a door in the back of my mind.

For a mouse, he's flamboyant—red shorts with big buttons, bulbous

yellow shoes good for a moon landing, and a dandy's white gloves.

He's cartoony, and his black eyes are spooky.

Did you ever notice... no pupils?

But his wide smile is so friendly and guileless I can't help but like him.

"Join the Merry Mouseketeers!" he calls earnestly, squeakily,

and I look at Annette Funicello and think, why not?

Now that the door is open, out steps Donna Reed,

It's a Wonderful Life glistening in her eyes,

Mom, Woman of Mystery

and I see she was really Jimmy Stewart's angel,

the girl-next-door, the ingénue

who stole soldiers' hearts during World War II,

and mine, and my friends' hearts as well.

More of my childhood tumbles out,

the Beav and Wally from *Leave It to Beaver*,

Bugs Bunny eating a carrot—"Ahhh, what's up, Doc?"—

Clark Kent tugging at his tie, almost trampling Sylvester

in his dash to a phone booth—"Suffering succotash!"—

and Elmer Fudd sputtering at that "wascally wabbit."

And then, thanks to Mr. Peabody's WABAC machine,

I am transported to Gram and Gramp's livingroom,

sprawled on the rug watching the two-knob, black and white T.V.,

and I see Clark Kent again, transformed,

"… a strange visitor from another planet."

"It's a bird! It's a plane! No! It's Superman!" shouts the crowd.

Locomotive strong, bullet-fast, N.B.A. jumping ability…

I'm young and in love with heroes and would be him if I could.

Cap Pistols, Cardboard Sleds & Seven Rusty Nails

Only, I can't. Mom calls us to supper.

Brother Scott drops from Tarzan's tree.

Duncan throws the spear he has fashioned for a Zulu battle.

I stop, mid-sprint, and lower my outstretched arms.

I will leap over a tall building tomorrow.

We leave the fireflies winking in the dusk.

Even heroes must eat.

Now, an old boy of sixty-six,

I lie in bed waiting for Sand Man

to sprinkle sleep dust in my eyes.

I hear Willie Winkie running in the street.

In the idle, discovering way I once had,

I wonder, can I open the door at will?

If I can, what will I find behind it?

I tiptoe down the stairs and call to Willie.

"Pssst. Come here," I whisper.

I show him the heavy latch made for giants, and we lift it together.

Straining our muscles mightily, we open the creaking, oaken door.

Mom, Woman of Mystery

The sounds of feasting float toward us on the cool evening air,

the clink of cutlery, the merry laughter of revelers, the songs of yore.

Willie and I slip across the threshold and creep forward.

At a table so long we can't see the other end, sit Rocky and Bullwinkle,

Robin Hood and Maid Marian, Ozzie and Harriet,

Tinkerbelle and Peter Pan, Marshall Dillon and Miss Kitty,

all the chimera who whisked me away on a magic carpet ride

night after halcyon night in 1950s America.

I feel a cold nose against my cheek and I gasp—it's Lassie! Suddenly,

the tumult dies down and Timmy calls clearly.

"Come home, Lassie! Come home!" His plaintive voice

and Lassie's tug on my sleeve pull me into the light.

Willie turns away, back to the streets of town,

but I go to the table, Lassie leading me like a seeing-eye dog.

Cheers fly skyward like sparks off a fire,

and in the midst of the lovely roar, of claps on the back,

and welcoming laughter from my incorporeal heroes,

the door slowly closes without a sound.

Cap Pistols, Cardboard Sleds & Seven Rusty Nails

The light spirals into the Looney Tunes shrinking iris,

and in the darkness, I vanish into memory, into Einstein time,

into the future that is now, and the now that was,

and, Janus-headed, I am looking forward and backward

and in all directions at once, and I meet the boy I was.

He runs through a meadow of fireflies,

a jar of twinkling lights in his hand.

An old school bell rings, and he turns and gazes

at the house silhouetted against the blue-back sky atop the hill.

A voice filled with love calls to us, "Supper's ready."

He stops and sees me, and he runs again, but to me now,

and throws his arms around me and hugs me.

Then, he takes my hand and leads me home.

❖

Mom, Woman of Mystery

CHAPTER 4

The Millhand and the Teacher

If Dad and Mom were the Sun and Moon in our childhood, Gramp and Gram Hastings were our Mars and Venus, meaning they lived next door and also exerted a strong, daily influence on our lives. Of course, Gram and Gramp Shattler mattered to us as well, but they were more like Saturn. Because they lived far away in Amesbury, Massachusetts, their pull wasn't quite as strong as that of our Hastings grandparents.

Mom and Dad's decision to move with Gram and Gramp Hastings to Happy Valley for our tadpole years between 1952 and '64 probably affected us boys as much as any other decision they made. I can hear Grammy singing, and I can see Gramp grinning crookedly even now, and I remember their special presence in my life even though it's been many years since they passed. Time. It creeps up on a person. I have watched the wrinkles appear on my face in the morning mirror, have watched them multiply, and it has dawned on me—over time—that I have crossed a threshold and reached the age Gram and Gramp were when I knew them as

Gramp and Gram Hastings with grandsons, Alec and Scott. It must be Sunday. Is that the West Lebanon church in the background?

a boy. How remarkable it is that I can remember them so clearly. When I look at photographs of them taken in their youth, I can't help but wish I could step into the picture and get to know them in that time—for just a little while.

Since I don't have a super power that will allow me to step into a picture, I'll talk about the Gram and Gramp I did know. All my early memories of them are entwined with their home and the 125 acres of woods and fields that was the known world when we were boys.

The Millhand and the Teacher

In a spiffy, three-piece wool suit with a newsboy hat in hand, Gramp stands with his arms around his friends. I would guess this picture was taken in the 1920s when he worked at the East Ryegate Paper Mill. Both my grandfathers were millhands. This photo might have been taken near the mill because the railroad tracks ran past it along the Vermont bank of the Connecticut River. What was the occasion, I wonder? Again, it was probably a Sunday because I imagine he worked every other day.

Josephine Hastings, née Giuseppina Antonia Teresa Fontana, 1901-1992. Gram was about to attend the Alumni Dinner & Dance after her graduation from Spaulding High School on June 19, 1919. Soon, she would be teaching in a one-room schoolhouse in Ryegate, Vermont, and within a few years from the date of this picture, Jo, the teacher, and Scott, the millhand, would meet and marry.

Here is one such memory, and it may be my earliest. We are still living with Gram and Gramp in the old, white clapboard farmhouse. After supper, we go out to the vegetable garden beyond the spot where the Harvey's barn once stood. All that is left of the barn—destroyed

Alec, Scott, and two unknown girls pretending to ride iron horses on the old foundation.

years before in a fire—is the weathered concrete foundation where weeds have taken root in cracks and rusty railings remain bolted to the concrete where they once separated the cows' stanchions.

It is late summer. I know this because the hay stands above my head. The grownups are picking corn, and we will have to help shuck it tomorrow on the porch so Mom and Gram can freeze it in blue, waxboard cartons. But right now, they have left us on our own. We bend hanks of hay toward each other and somehow tie them in the middle to make circular grass huts like the ones we saw in *National Geographic* magazine. We speed-crawl on our hands and knees from one hut to another on narrow paths invisible from ten feet away. The golden light lingers. The summer evening is warm and windless. Finally, the sun sinks below Blake Hill. Twilight comes, and we go indoors. I remember a sense of the idyllic out there in the field without, at that time, even knowing the word. Back at the house—and this makes me chuckle—I remember Gramp walking up the plank ramp to the backroom and thumping the heel of his hand on the door jamb. It was his way to call General, his cat. General was a friendly, tiger-striped tomcat who took evening walks out by the garden with a doe. The doe, I'm sure, came to check on the Hastings' vegetables.

The Millhand and the Teacher

During those early years, when hay could still grow higher than my head, Grammy had a lot to do with making that small world seem idyllic. By the time I met her (and was old enough to remember her), she was a pleasantly plump woman in her mid-fifties with an inviting smile and bright, kind eyes. I think the dish of ice cream she and Gramp enjoyed every night had something to do with plumpness for both of them. I don't remember ever seeing her in slacks, which is what people back then often called pants when women wore them. She may have worn skirts, but in the picture my mind sends me, she is always wearing a dress. If she was "going out," she wore nylon stockings, clip-on earrings, and perhaps a brooch. She always carried a pocketbook.

Gram didn't go places by herself. When she was coming of age, cars weren't yet in common use, and as a teacher in a one-room schoolhouse, boarding with her students' families, she had little use for one. By the time cars did become commonplace, she was the mother of two young children and, knowing Gram, not much inclined toward driving. Cars back then were not the machines of convenience we know today. Cranking a car engine to start it broke many a wrist, and even if you got your flivver on the road, the roads themselves were no picnic. Horses and cars shared them—not always successfully—and if you think potholes and mud are a problem in Vermont today, well, as Gramp might say, "you don't know the half of it."

Yes, Grammy was almost always at home when we lived in Happy Valley. She was just over fifty when we moved there, and I imagine the mile-long walk to the village of Taftsville didn't appeal to her. I don't remember that she minded being home. If the farm was our world, I think it was also hers. I never heard her complain about being "stuck" there. In fact, I don't remember her complaining about much of anything. Years later, I marveled at this, especially when I learned that she had lost both her parents by the time she was ten.

When Mom went to work at the Woodstock Pharmacy, Gram happily took on the challenging task of overseeing her three, mischievous young grandsons, and we happily looked forward to seeing her every day when school got out. Ken Barrup drove the white Checker cab that doubled as a school bus for Fred Doubleday's taxi service. He picked us up every morning at the foot of the hill below our house and dropped us off at Gram and Gramp's in the afternoon. Those afternoons with Gram are a fond memory. By the time we arrived at her door, her kitchen woodbox was running low, so we would bring in armloads of stovewood from the shed. The woodshed was home to a tribe of charming cats who always made this chore a little more exciting by hissing and spitting if we got too close. After filling the box, we sat on the gray bench next to the massive, cast-iron cookstove and used Gramp's bootjack to pull off our boots. Then, we lifted the lid on the bench and dropped them into the storage space underneath.

We took off the wool mittens Mom or Gram had knit for us. Because we had been playing King of the Mountain at school (pig pile!), building snowmen, and maybe even packing a few snowballs, our mittens were wet, so we hung them on a wooden rack by the hot water tank at the back of the stove. Then, we hung up our coats and were ready to bask in the warmth and intoxicating smells of Gram's kitchen. Some days there was fresh bread coming out of the oven. My God, the aroma! And always there were cookies. Gram kept the cookie jar full of toll house cookies, ginger snaps, date-filled cookies, sour cream cookies, cookies of all kinds. We sat around the claw-foot, oak table, and Gram served us milk and those delicious cookies from the special cookie jar she kept on the counter. It's not surprising that I can describe that jar down to the smallest detail. Inside was the stuff dreams are made of! It was shaped like an apple

Grammy loved to sing. Judging by the footlights, it was a public performance.

and painted apple-red and yellow. It had two green leaves in relief on top, and from them protruded a stem which served as a handle by which the lid could be lifted and the contents inspected and sniffed. When Duncan, Denise, and I visited Scott and his wife Susan in Charles Town, West Virginia a few years ago, Duncan found a cookie jar just like that one in a local antique store.

From left, three of Grammy's older sisters, Aunt Rosa, Aunt Mickey (Michelina), and Aunt Annie. Probably this picture was taken in Barre, Vermont not long before their mother died in 1911. Aunt Rosa, the oldest, was nineteen when Adele Rossi Fontana passed away, and she took Grammy under her care. Their father, Santino, who worked in the Barre granite sheds, died of silicosis at 39 in 1904.

Grammy was always a comforting presence for me. I would walk through the backroom, past Gramp's workbench (the repository of nuts and bolts, myriad jars of nails, the odd handsaw or hammer, spare fishing line, and a million other whatnots), past the freezer chest stocked with our vegetables and the meats from some deal Gramp made, and through the kitchen door only to find Gram washing dishes in the sink and happily singing a song from long ago like "The Sidewalks of New York." She had a lovely, lovely voice and could keep herself pleasant company on the piano. It is only in my later years that I have paused to think about her warm-hearted, loving manner and wonder if it came, at least in part, from her Italian parents and perhaps a culturally different upbringing. What a sad thing to be orphaned so young. It is no surprise that family was everything to her, and that she was very attached to her sisters. How brave Gram was to become a teacher and go out into the world after such a loss!

Gramp's life was no picnic either. Memory plays its tricks, but I think he was working for a farmer named Hod Gleason by the time he was eleven years old. He was mucking out cows and doing all the scut work, but he was getting paid and he took pride in that. According to family lore, his father, Oliver, showed up in the spring and brought him home. He bought Gramp a mackinaw and a pair of boots from his wages and pocketed the rest, which was a parent's oft-exercised right in that time, although it probably felt unjust to Gramp. At fourteen, Gramp was working for the Connecticut Valley Lumber Company which had been owned by the famous (or infamous, depending on your slant) George Van Dyke. Really, he was working for an under-boss named Bill Yettin, and since he was too young to be a chopper, he was driving a team of horses and twitching logs out of the woods or driving log loads down to a landing. Driving those loads was no mean feat. The teamster was generally taking the logs downhill, sometimes on a steep grade, and Lord help you if the sled and horses got away from you. If the load flipped, all hell broke loose, and more than one team and their driver came to a bad end that way. It was a lot of responsibility for a kid.

Gramp was three years younger than Gram, but I always thought of him as older. When I was a boy, I have to admit, I was a little scared of him. I thought he was stern, and I was never quite sure of where I stood with him, but I also admired the hell out of him. He gave me my first beer. We were out in the bay of the woodshed where he parked the World War II surplus Willys Jeep that was the "workhorse" on the place, especially for the ongoing task of getting up on the hill to cut firewood and bring it home for June (Dad) to split. He handed me that beer in a juice glass from the kitchen. I was conscious even then that I was climbing another rung on the ladder of manhood. I never did take to cigarettes. He smoked Kent micronite filtered cigs, and I puffed on a smoldering butt he dropped in the yard one day, but I didn't like it a bit. That was fortunate. I read recently that the filters contained cancer-causing blue asbestos. The beer, though—I kind of liked that beer.

He also taught me to drive. At least, he tried. We had been up on the hill above the sugarhouse and the apple orchard with the Jeep, working up some firewood. I think we were going back down the hill for lunch, and if it was Saturday, he may have been hoping to watch the Red Sox and fall asleep in his recliner if they were losing, which was a better-than-even bet. He asked me if I wanted to drive, and I said, tentatively, "Okay."

"Push in the clutch and put it in second," he said. Then, he showed me the shifting pattern so I would know where second was. "Keep your hand on the shifter, and don't let it pop out of gear. The brakes are shot." Of course, I knew what the "brakes are shot" warning meant, but I wasn't quite sure how to avoid "popping out of gear." I soon found out. There was a steep hill going down from the sugarhouse. I kept my hand on the gearshift, but I was concentrating on manhandling the steering wheel to keep us in the tire tracks and nursing the gas pedal rather than goosing it. Then, we hit a bump, my hand lifted off the shifter for a mosquito sneeze, the shifter popped, and—holy moly!—out of second we went! Suddenly, we were picking up speed and bouncing down the hill hellbent for a wreck at the bottom. I don't remember much after that. I clung to the steering wheel for dear life and somehow kept the brakeless Jeep on the road without swerving too much or rolling over. We coasted to a stop at the bottom where the road took a slight up-swoop and then flattened out. Gramp took over without a word. I moved sheepishly to the passenger seat. That was the last driving lesson I got from Gramp.

As with Mom, Gramp was a mystery to me much of the time. Gram was an open book, always warm and affectionate, always easy to read, but I couldn't always tell what Gramp was thinking, and as I said, I tended to tread lightly in his presence, especially after the near crash of the Jeep. He could be talkative enough—depending on the subject—and I think, as a salesman, he must have often exercised his not inconsiderable skill as a raconteur while talking to customers, but he could also be closemouthed, and I don't remember him smiling a lot. No doubt that made him seem gruff when I was a lad. How much of his taciturn manner came from his Yankee upbringing, and how much was rooted in causes I knew nothing about, I can't say.

I'm sure his manner worked to his advantage at times. Duncan told me a story in which I suspect his steely gaze and unreadable expression were helpful. Selden Osmer owned a fairly large farm across the valley from us. Before I go any further, I should tell you I learned only recently that his full name was Selden. When I was a boy, everyone knew him as Si. Happy Valley Brook was the boundary of his property and Gramp's. Si raised pigs and sold them, we were told, to McKenzie Meats. He was not a great hand at mending his fences, and Gramp was getting tired of his hogs rooting up the Mooney Lot along the upper part of the brook because he rented that land as pasture for heifers. He may have had another concern about Si's pigs. Pigs are omnivorous. I didn't know it when I was a little fellow, but I learned later it wouldn't have been out of character for one of Si's five hundred-pound hogs to make a tasty meal of a small Hastings boy.

If I ever had any doubts about that, I had only to remember one of my early trips to Woodstock on my new, three-speed, English bicycle. When I pedaled by the abandoned Reed place, I saw a dead cow Si had dumped in the bushes just off the road. I closed my eyes quickly and opened them again. Was the cow moving? Did it just bulge upward? Suddenly, a litter of piglets spooked and ran squealing out of the cow's stomach where they had been feasting. Si was supposed to cook the meat he fed to the pigs, and he had the means to do it, but here was proof that he sometimes skipped that step. Anyway, I understood from that incident that meat was indeed meat, and—should the chance present itself—a pig would probably not turn up its nose at mine.

Gramp had asked Si to fix his fences more than once, but Si hadn't done it. His family had lived on their hillside farm for generations, so maybe he felt Gramp was an interloper in Happy Valley or maybe Si, like his livestock, was pig-headed. The truth is, I don't know what was going through Si's mind, but I do know Gramp finally got fed up. He put his deer rifle in the Jeep and rode up to Si's abode with Dunc along for company. There were pigs right in the backroom. He knocked on the door, shoved the pigs aside, and he and Dunc went into the kitchen. Si lived in the house with his mother, an old woman by that time, and they were both at home.

Adding to the odor of pigs on the hillside was a dump site just down the lane from the house. Si had arranged with the Town of Woodstock for residents to dump their garbage on a piece of his land at the head of Happy Valley Brook. The rats in that part of town stood up on their haunches, put their noses in the air, sniffed eagerly, and scurried off in the direction of the new dump as fast as their four legs would carry them. They must have thought they'd died and gone to heaven. Plenty of the townspeople brought their small caliber rifles to the dump to practice their marksmanship and keep the population at bay, but there always seemed to be plenty of rats left after target practice was over.

In the dump's early days, the trash was burned, and it didn't make for a pleasant summer evening when the smoke drifted down through Happy Valley to the Hastings' neighborhood. Granny Osmer used to pick the dump for goodies, and one day she fell through a section that had live coals underneath. She got seriously burned, and wasn't spry enough afterward to vault over fences the way she used to do. Dad often had nicknames for people, and he called her Granny Grunt. That may sound unkind, but he always smiled just a little when he said it, and I think it signaled his mixture of amusement and disbelieving admiration when he thought of the life led by Si and his mother and their hired hand Vilas Bridge, whom Dad called Virus because—as he claimed—there was not a germ on earth that could get the better of him. I think Dad's qualified admiration of Vilas and the Osmers was for their remarkable hardiness and self-reliance.

Apparently, Si became something of a local legend after my brothers and I grew up and left Woodstock. Over the years, more and more people moved to Woodstock from out of state, and I suppose he represented a fast-disappearing breed, a thrifty farmer whose old-fashioned, rural values appealed to urban refugees disenchanted with a glut of plastic, pavement, and growing pollution. He must have seemed like an authentic, even appealing, Vermont character. He was definitely authentic, but when I remember my own encounters with Si, well, I can only say that those who knew him from a distance might have found him less appealing up close.

I was certainly influenced by my elders' thoughts about Si, but I ran into him many times myself and had some basis for my own opinion. Because Dick Watson was my best friend, and because I was conducting a long-term taste test of all the different candy bars at the Watson's Country Store, I stopped there often. Si also frequented the store to pick up this and that on his way home, and he would stay to visit with Harvey Watson, the owner and Dick's dad. When I opened the heavy front door, and the bell tinkled, I always knew immediately if Si was present. The odor of pig manure and other pungent smells that followed him everywhere was enough to gag a maggot as Dad used to say. My hankering for my favorite Hollywood candy bar would quickly fade, and like as not, I would let the door swing shut again, go sit on the porch bench, and wait for Si to leave. Don't get me wrong. The noxious cloud Si trailed in his wake was not what really put me off. Heck, I shoveled plenty of cow manure as a kid (though—if one can be a snob about manure—it smelled better). I was wary of Si for some other reason, but it's hard to put my finger on it. Ironically, it might have been—as with Gramp—that it was hard to tell what he was thinking. But with Si, I felt that if I did know, I might not like it. Maybe he saw me as one of Scott Hastings' kids and was as suspicious of me as I was of him. Who knows?

His own wariness would have been understandable because the Hastings and Si had, what might be called today, some unresolved issues. I've already mentioned the poor state of his fences which allowed his hogs to root up the Mooney Lot. On top of that, his dump polluted the brook. We fished that brook—Gramp stocked it with trout—and we swam in the Big Pool down below Gram and Gramp's house. That is, we did until Dad got polio. That's when we learned that a lot of the garbage from Si's dump was contaminating the brook, and that it was probably the cause of Dad's illness. Our doctor thought I might have polio too, and at Dartmouth Hitchcock Hospital a very long, thick needle was inserted between my vertebrae to withdraw spinal fluid and check for the disease. Fortunately, I didn't have it.

Anyway, I've wandered afield again. To get back to the Osmer's house, I don't know if the cookstove had fallen through the kitchen floor by that time, but if it hadn't, it did eventually. Dunc must have enjoyed looking around, though, while Gramp parleyed with Si. The dilapidated house contained Osmer artifacts that dated back generations. According to Pearl Watson's local history book, *Taftsville Tales*, one of Si's ancestors was a colonial ranger during the French and Indian War, and Si still had his powder horn.

That didn't cut any ice with Gramp. He had similar Yankee roots, and he was losing patience with Si.[4] As I understand it, he told Si if he didn't see him down at the brook fixing fence within a half hour, he would shoot any pig he saw on his land. In the old days, a hog reeve would have impounded the hogs, and Si would have had to pay a fine to get them back, but hog reeves were a relic of the past. So, Gramp and Dunc drove back to Happy Valley Road and parked where they had a clear view down to the brook. Sure enough, there were hogs down there rooting around in our pasture. Gramp waited the half hour, and when Si didn't show, he rested his thirty-ought-six on the hood of the Jeep,

---

[4] The inscription on Si's powderhorn said it was made at Fort Edward during the French and Indian War in 1758. Coincidentally, Gramp's fifth great uncle, Jonas Hastings, fought at the Battle of Lake George (vicinity of Fort Edward) in 1755.

took careful aim, and pulled the trigger. One of the hogs dropped in its tracks. No doubt, Si heard the shot and investigated because the holes in the fence were fixed pronto. It's more than likely that he also skinned the pig and saved the meat.

If relations between Si and the Hastings were strained at times, I can at least say I enjoyed the company of Si's brother Pete. Here again, I learned only recently that Pete was another Osmer known by a nickname. His real name was Arthur. He built a small, frame cabin on Osmer land along Happy Valley Road in the early sixties. The cabin was only big enough for a steel cot, a small box stove, and room to turn yourself around. Pete was an older man by then, and he spent most of his time hunting and fishing. He was often outside sawing stovewood with a bow saw when I rode by on my bike. I would stop to visit if I wasn't in a hurry. Pete could talk your ear off if you didn't know how to make an exit, but he could also be entertaining. His cantankerous manner was leavened by a sense of humor and a wealth of tales, some only barely believable.

Once when I stopped, he was gimping around on a crutch and splitting kindling. He had been out deer hunting one day and met up with one of the boys from Taftsville. Sadly, the boy was also hunting and had left the safety off on his rifle. I don't know

Scott Edison Hastings, Senior, 1904-1991. Gramp is posing on the roof the boardinghouse where he rented a room while working at the East Ryegate Paper Mill in the 1920s.

how it happened, but the gun went off and Pete was shot in the foot. He spent a day or two at the hospital in Hanover, but he said he got impatient with those "pinhead doctors" and left. He hitchhiked home and went back to his usual routines, but infection must have set in. I heard he died not long after that. Years later I stopped by the cabin site. The cabin was long gone, but I found his bow saw rusting under a layer of pine needles. I brought it home and hung it on the side of my shed in remembrance of Pete, one of those crusty old coots I knew as a boy.

Yes, Gramp was taciturn, but as this story suggests, if he didn't say a lot, he certainly meant what he did say. He had a high opinion of Duncan even as a youngster, for he would never have taken him along to Si's otherwise. They were great pals. They spent many hours together on weekends working in the woodlot and on Gramp's other projects. I think Gramp recognized in him a kindred spirit. It is probably no coincidence that Duncan became the hunter in the family and the one who loved to boil sap, saw lumber, and hammer out iron on an anvil. The two of them were made from the same Yankee mold—independent, self-reliant, ingenious, thrifty men who were particularly fond of working with their hands.

In the picture (p.117), Gramp is neatly dressed, and—to me—he looks like someone who could sell you something, which is what he did most of his life. I think brother Scott bears an uncanny resemblance to him, the same intriguing, sly smile and sometimes ironic sense of humor, the same gift of gab, the same sharp mind. I remember Scott telling a Francis Colburn story at my niece Maria's wedding years ago. It was a long story and a challenging one to recite. It was the one about the cyclist and ended with the line, "it is better to have *peedaled* backwards than never to have *peedaled* at all." He told it as if Francis was sitting on his shoulder whispering in his ear, and it was a damned impressive feat of memory and storytelling. Gramp was that kind of storyteller. My God, when he and Dad and Uncle Bob got around the kitchen table in Grammy's kitchen and began spinning tales, we boys were all ears.

Gramp may not have graduated from high school, but he was as smart as a whip, and he had sand. When he was in his late teens or early twenties, pulpwood jammed on the river at the mill in Ryegate. None of the older, wiser men wanted to climb out on those four-foot lengths of wood and place dynamite to blow the tangle apart. They knew the danger. At any moment the river current could cause the whole shebang to shift, and if a fella lost his footing, he could be ground into hamburger. Gramp volunteered to do the job. I imagine the other men were skeptical, and maybe some tried to talk him out of it. No dice. He went to the blacksmith and asked him to hammer out a pair of iron cleats he could strap to his sneakers. With those on his feet and a stick of dynamite on a pole, he scrambled out on the jam and put that stick where it would do the most good. Then, he unspooled some fuse and lit it. The logs blew, the jam cleared, and he went off about his business. When I remember him now, I think of him as an entirely unflappable character, and maybe that was part and parcel of all he had done and all he had seen over the course of a century that saw the advent of cars, airplanes, the radio, television, the Great Depression, World Wars I and II, The Korean War, the Civil Rights Movement, the Vietnam War, and a man walking on the moon.

His end epitomized his personality. He learned that he had a spot on one of his lungs. It was cancer, probably from that damned micronite filter (along with tobacco tar, of course). He made preparations to ensure Gram's comfort, and then he continued with as normal a life as he could. He tended his hollyhocks and sent me home with logging chains, an old railroad lantern, an axe, and so on as he began clearing the cellar of the flotsam and jetsam of a lifetime. And he waited. One night a year or so later he fell asleep in his armchair watching television, which was a long-established routine by then. But that night he didn't wake up again and go to bed with Gram as he usually did. No muss, no fuss, he left us on his own terms, and Gram followed a year later.

The Millhand and the Teacher

Gramp Hastings with grandson Duncan.

I learned a great deal from both of them. When they say the apple doesn't fall too far from the tree, they mean that children cannot help but carry a great deal of their parents with them even as they walk their own road. In our case—and I think my brothers would agree—we have carried with us a great deal we learned from our grandparents as well.

❖

CHAPTER 5

How the Hastings Boys Became Bookworms

"What was one of your favorite stories as a child?" When this question landed in my inbox this morning, I was reading a passage from a wonderful author named Ivan Doig. The following excerpt from his novel, *The Whistling Season*, strikes me as true and also as a good springboard to launch this chapter: "The Rembrandt light of memory [is] finicky and magical and faithful at the same time... I have learned to rely on a certain radiance of detail to bring back the exactitude of a moment."

If I shine a Rembrandt light on the Hastings family's encounters with reading, I see a few of them with exactitude. I see, for instance, Mom tucking us into bed, planting a goodnight kiss on our foreheads, and leaving Dad seated in a chair about to open a book under the light of a bedside lamp. As Mom's footsteps retreat down the stairs, I squint at the book's cover.

"What is this story about?" I ask.

"It's about a bear named Winnie-the-Pooh."

"Oh. Can I see the cover?" I ask.

I wondered if I would like the book. I wasn't sure Pooh was a good name for a hero, and there could be no doubt he was the hero of the book if his name was on the cover. But then, I trusted Dad, so I decided to listen and give Pooh a chance. Dad held the book up so I could see the illustration. The picture showed a bear—presumably Pooh—standing on his hind legs with arms akimbo. He was looking at a gray donkey who, in turn, was inspecting a crockery pot at the bear's feet. Standing to one side of the bear was a small animal with pointy ears. I would soon learn that the perpetually gloomy donkey was named Eeyore, and the pointy-eared, timid little friend of Pooh's was Piglet. The piece of crockery was a honey pot. Pooh was, indeed, the likable, but unlikely hero of these stories. I say unlikely because even he called himself a "bear of little brain," and it was hard for me to imagine a hero with little brain. He did have a lot of heart, however. He was kind and generous. His only real failing was a too-great love of honey, but perhaps this can be forgiven since he was a bear, and all bears love honey.

As it turned out, I loved *Winnie-the-Pooh*. I remember once, as a teacher, hearing that my students might not remember all I taught them, but they would remember

How the Hastings Boys Became Bookworms

the kind of person I was. That was a valuable truth to learn, and interestingly, it has been my experience with books as well. I don't remember everything Pooh did, but I will always remember Pooh himself. I learned from hearing the story of this amiable bear that heroes don't always carry six-shooters and run off rustlers. Sometimes they are just ordinary folk who make all our lives better because of their friendship and their cheerful outlook on the world. "What?" you ask. "Nothing of the story itself?" Well, no, because I wouldn't deprive you of the pleasure of spending a day with Pooh if you never have. But I will say this. Whenever I think of the day Pooh and Piglet tracked the Heffalump or the day Pooh got his head stuck inside a honey jar or the day Tigger arrived, I remember that Mr. Milne was a cracking good storyteller, and suddenly I am eager to read his books again and return with you to Pooh Corner.

In those early reading experiences, the pictures were almost as important as the story. When I see Pooh and his friends in my mind's eye, they are always the figures I remember from Ernest Shepard's illustrations. And when I see Rat, Mole, and Toad from *The Wind in the Willows,* *they* are indelibly Shepard's creations too. This love of illustration was shared by Scott and Duncan. I'm sure Dad helped inspire our appreciation. He learned to draw as a boy and continued to use that skill all his life. He had a collection of prints showing men of Britain's Scottish regiments in uniform. One of his early drawing projects was to do a set of meticulous pen-and-ink drawings using those prints as guides. I remember his love of Arthur Rackham's work and the work of all the other artists of the Golden Age of Illustration. This may explain why, even after setting Pooh aside in search of stories with more swashbuckling action, we continued to read books with lots of pictures.

These were the so-called comic books, and we encountered them in the late '50s at the tail end of their own golden age. Really, they were thin, soft-cover magazines that could be read in a single sitting. They were cheap and wildly popular with kids who yearned for the stories of super heroes like Batman, Spiderman, the Fantastic Four, the X-Men, and—no surprise—Superman. We collected these mags, hid them in our bedrooms, posted NO TRESPASSING signs on our doors, and always read them with one ear cocked for the sound of an intruder. All this caution was necessary, of course, because comic books had been known to walk off and disappear only to be found later in someone else's bedroom.

Talk about role models, those super heroes really embodied that American notion that, "you can do anything if you put your mind to it." I can still see one of my favorites, the Flash, running so fast he became a blur. Wow! I often wished *I* could run that fast. Maybe if I had just tried harder? Eventually, we set our comic books aside with other "childish things," but I still enjoy stories with pictures, and I know my brothers do. Scott told me that he read Jane Porter's book, *The Scottish Chiefs*, in its entirety while waiting at the hospital for his daughter Asia to be born. I remember that book too, and I particularly remember the cover art by N.C. Wyeth. Wyeth also illustrated *Treasure Island* and *Robin Hood*, two of my favorites.

But I'm getting ahead of myself. The day came when we brothers learned to read on our own, and as Duncan said, the nightly bedtime story came to a screeching halt. By then, Dad had finished building our house in Happy Valley. He was getting Hastings Highland House off the ground, and Mom was constantly cooking, cleaning, canning, freezing, weeding, preserving, knitting, mending, and doing God only knows how many other chores. I can imagine them downstairs the first night all three of us were able to read ourselves to sleep, Dad whispering to Mom, "Thank God!" It must have been a relief, finally, for them to tuck us in, and instead of sitting down to read about Toad stealing a car and going to prison in *The Wind in the Willows*, being able to say, "Okay, you can read until eight o'clock. Then, lights out, and no monkey business!"

And I think it was fine with us. We inherited *en masse* the books Dad read as a boy. When I talked with Duncan and Scott about these books, we reeled off a list of titles as if we'd read them yesterday: *The Motorboat Boys on the Columbia River*, *The Boy Allies in Belgium*, *The Hardy Boys and the Tower Mystery* (or any other number of mysteries), *Tom Swift and His Flying Machine*, *Tom Slade on the River*, *Tarzan and the Jewels of Opar*, and so on. I remember *Rebecca of Sunnybrook Farm*, which seemed like an outlier amongst all the others, but I suspect it was Mom's, and she hoped against hope that one of us might adopt one of her childhood favorites.

At any rate, we took up reading with all the same fervor we expended on building secret forts, digging tunnels through snowbanks, mining garnets from the stonewall next to the house, adopting frogs in the eight-foot dimple of a pond in the old brickyard next door, and climbing trees (especially the forbidden one close to the house but out of sight of Mom's kitchen window). Sometimes we read after curfew with flashlights. Most nights we conked out quickly after a day of nonstop bike riding, ball playing, wrestling, sword fighting, or tobogganing. Duncan and I fondly remember the shelves Dad built into the knee wall of the upstairs

How the Hastings Boys Became Bookworms

bedroom we shared. We stored many treasures on those shelves (including my sea shell collection), but the books—within easy reach of our beds—took up most of that space. Stretched out comfortably under the covers, our heads propped up on pillows, our gooseneck lamps fastened to the headboard and shining on the page, we read and read, began finally to yawn, and slipped into dreamland while Mom and Dad enjoyed a peaceful, uninterrupted evening downstairs. Those bookshelves—good idea, Mom and Dad!

After we exhausted the small library we had inherited from Dad, the folks put Plan B into action. Plan B was designed to further our education and continue entertaining us in the evenings. We began weekly visits to Woodstock's Norman Williams Public Library, a routine that lasted for years. While Mom and Dad visited the grownup's section, we explored the Children's Room where—eureka!—we discovered the *Freddy the Pig* books. I say "we," but certainly it was Scott, the oldest, who discovered Freddy first, and Duncan and I fell in line afterward as fans of these wonderful books in which Freddy was a pilot nonpareil, a dexterous magician (even with trotters), a detective equal to Sherlock Holmes, and always the hero called on to match wits with the villainous Simon, wily leader of a gang of criminal rats.

The Norman Williams Public Library, a portal to the unknown worlds and delights found in the pages of books (photo courtesy of Woodstock History Center).

To my mind, the library, built in 1883 by brothers Norman and Edward Williams on the site of their parents' former home and given to the town in their parents' honor, was more like a church than the one we attended every Sunday. It must have been tempting for the townies to play hopscotch on the three-foot squares of slate which paved the walk to its front door, but I don't remember ever seeing any chalk marks there. Perhaps a sense of being close to something special kept such desecration to a minimum. We had to climb several sets of granite steps to reach the portico. Not long ago, I stood on the top step and thought about the

How the Hastings Boys Became Bookworms

architect's design, how it could make a newly arriving patron feel... what? A little elevated? A little removed from the pedestrian world of the sidewalk? Most of all, perhaps, a little excited at being on the threshold of discovery? For that's what all those books just beyond the door represented to me.

 Remembering its sills of Barre granite, the walls of red stone from Burlington, the roof of dark gray Poultney slate, I hear a voice I might have heard as boy. It says, "you are about to enter a citadel of knowledge, a place where the dead can speak, ... so go quietly please." Back then, each time I passed through the Roman arches framing the entrance, I could just as well have been stepping into Wells' time machine, for on the other side of the door I might encounter Natty Bumpo or King Arthur or mad Captain Ahab. The place was otherworldly for me. It was no coincidence that the length of the building (the nave) corresponded to the long axis of a Christian cross, and the two side wings (transepts) to the horizontal axis. This cruciform layout was typical of medieval cathedrals. Oak trusses soared upward to a ceiling so high it was lost in shadows. Heavy chandeliers suspended from that ceiling lit enormous oak tables topped in red leather. Beautifully crafted cases displayed samurai swords, exquisite Japanese ivory carvings, and a small, life-like Japanese man clad in a loincloth and pulling a rickshaw. I learned while writing this chapter that Edward Williams traveled the world as a railroad tycoon, collected these *objets d'art*, and willed them to his daughter Anna Williams Dreer upon his death. She generously donated them to the library for the benefit of Woodstock's children.

With all its architectural majesty and beautiful furnishings, the library was, indeed, a sanctum for Woodstock's children, a place that inspired not only awe but also contemplation. No doubt this was by design. Of course, being young, my brothers and I and our friends didn't stay awed forever. Not so many years later, we were meeting high school girls at those giant oak tables and being hushed by the white-haired librarian for making too much noise. Still, it remains a hallowed place in my memory, a place where my brothers and I pushed beyond the boundaries of Happy Valley into worlds beyond.

I hope all this gives you a sense of how the Hastings boys became bookworms. In the end Dad was our greatest source of inspiration in this department. Gramp read Zane Grey's and Louis Lamour's westerns, and also the newspaper almost exclusively. By the time he dropped into his recliner at the end of a work day, I imagine he was just happy to rest, to watch *Gunsmoke* or

How the Hastings Boys Became Bookworms

the Red Sox, read an escapist novel, and maybe nod off for a while. Like many Vermonters of his generation, he was already working hard by the age of eleven. Money was scarce and savings even scarcer.

Mom and Gram read the *Ladies Home Journal* and *Good Housekeeping*, and in the sixties the family also had subscriptions to magazines like *National Geographic*, *Time* and *Life*. *Life* was famous for its photographs depicting current events around the world. Mom and Gram worked almost all of their waking hours trying to keep the family fed, clothed, and comfortable, so reading must have presented a dilemma. I'm sure they believed in its value, but they must have been torn between that belief and the oft-held view that reading was a bit frivolous. Who had time?

Dad, however, was a special case. He worked as hard or harder than anyone else in the family, but he still found time to read. No doubt Gram encouraged him as a boy—she was a teacher herself, after all—or maybe books and knowledge just attracted him like a gigantic electro-magnet. Whatever the reason, he was a voracious reader with catholic tastes all his life. He was a great fan of the Sherlock Holmes stories, the works of Rudyard Kipling, *The Seven Pillars of Wisdom*, and countless other books, fiction and nonfiction, and his enthusiasm for reading was infectious. I remember him saying once that you can teach yourself almost anything if you know how to read. I have always found that advice useful even though today that reading might be done online rather than in the pages of a book. I am grateful to him for turning me into a bookworm, and I'm sure Scott and Duncan are grateful as well.

❖

How the Hastings Boys Became Bookworms

CHAPTER 6

"You're Not the Boss of Me!"

I want to tell you about the many bosses who "employed" me when I was a whippersnapper. I'll even tell you about one or two of my own efforts to be a boss. Memories of the 1950s and '60s come to me willy-nilly, the smell of Gram's fresh-baked bread coming out of the oven of the wood-fired cookstove, one of Dad's pet sayings like "that fella doesn't know enough to ache," or the sound of baseball cards flapping against the spokes of my bike wheels. Some of these memories have stuck to me like glue while others, alas, have gone "down the tubes" (another of Dad's sayings). If you'll humor me, I'll unspool these memories of bosses not as a story, but as they come to me, a parade of characters who peopled the world of my childhood.

One of my first bosses was Mom, Elsie Richards Hastings. I'm going to make a minor correction here based on input from my older brother Scott. Mom was *the* boss. I gave my mother a hard time right from the beginning because I let it be known that I wanted to join the family during a snowstorm five days before

The Boss in 1947, two years before the arrival of her first employee, Scott Oliver Hastings. It's easy to see why Dad fell in love.

Christmas in 1951. It was my first attempt at being a little boss, and I managed to get my way. Mom had to go to the Newport hospital by taxi in the middle of the night. Mom, Dad and two-year-old Scott were living in an apartment in Newport, New Hampshire because Dad had recently graduated from Keene State Teachers College and had his first job teaching "shop" there in Newport. A couple years ago, Duncan and

"You're Not the Boss of Me!"

I found the old New England house where they lived on a street not far from the school. It looked quite dignified when we saw it, with two full stories and the usual white clapboards, but maybe it wasn't as well kept in 1951. Mom and Dad said they stored shoes by the bed to throw at the rats that scurried across the floor at night in search of crumbs in the apartment kitchen. The rats' dining opportunities must have been limited because I'm sure Mom was a fastidious housekeeper even then.

No doubt they were planning their future because Dad soon took a new teaching post in Hartford, Vermont, and in 1952 they moved with Gram and Gramp to an old farm about a mile up the road from Watson's Country Store in Taftsville. This was home for Scott, Duncan, and me until we moved to Woodstock in 1964. Back then, it seemed a place as large as the Louisiana Purchase.

But hey, here I am, off on a tangent again. I'm supposed to be telling you about Mom, my first boss. We moved to the old farm that had belonged to the Harvey family since 1783. Marion Harvey had to sell the property after her husband Ray died of a heart attack. Leaving the home that had been in the Harvey family for so long must have been sad. Little did I know that my life would become entwined with the lives of two Harvey descendants. Ray and Marion's niece, Patricia Harvey spent her summers at the farm while growing up. She eventually married Fred Doubleday and settled in Woodstock. Their son Fred became one of my closest friends during high school, and Fred's oldest brother David also became a close friend in the '70s and remains my friend to this day.

Mom and Dad had an upstairs bedroom in the farmhouse, the one above the two figures on the lawn (opposite page). Gram and Gramp had the upstairs bedroom in the gable above the picket fence. I'm not sure where Scott was sleeping when we moved in, but he would have been four, so he may have had the room with the two twin beds and the very desirable cowboy wallpaper. Yours truly was stationed in a crib next to Mom and Dad's bedroom door.

Here's the bossing part. Every afternoon I was supposed to take a nap. You know how it is. The day comes when a kid doesn't want to nap anymore and gets the message across by crying or having some other form of baby meltdown. On that day, I decided. No more naps! I waited until Mom left, and once I could no longer hear her shoes whispering on the carpeted stairs, I got up on my hands and knees, grabbed the spindles of the crib frame, and banged my head

Gram and Gramp's house (formerly the Harvey farm, a.k.a. Happy Valley Farm) complete with laundry hanging on the porch.

against the headboard. I did this with such enthusiasm that I got the whole thing rocking. I'm sure Mom came running up the stairs to find out what the heck all the racket was about.

I don't know if there was a second head-banging session, but knowing the Hastings' reputation for being a little muley, I suspect there may have been one or two more. I also don't know if the boss gave me

Scott and Alec, two old hands in their cowboy outfits, complete with six shooters.

a swat on my behind for these antics, but it's entirely possible because, back then, a person's backside was still considered a prime place to deliver a lesson. I'm pretty sure about one thing. The afternoon naps didn't last much longer. Eventually, I not only left the afternoon nap behind, I left the crib entirely and moved into Scott's bedroom, the one with the cowboy wallpaper! I loved to lie in bed on a summer night when it was still twilight outside, look at the

"You're Not the Boss of Me!"

pictures of the cowboys, and imagine myself roping calves or fighting off rustlers with my six-gun.

On a slight detour, and in fairness to the adult bosses of my childhood, I must acknowledge that my brothers and I were ourselves bosses. I know this because I distinctly remember a phrase we used over and over: "Don't boss me around!" My daughter Calley coined her own version of this phrase a generation later when she said, for the first but not the last time, "You're not the boss of me!" This suggests that bosses can be found everywhere as we know from old proverbs like "Too many cooks spoil the soup" and "Too many chiefs, not enough Indians." My brothers and I didn't have much success bossing each other, but we did get some practice with our dog Spike, a good-natured dog if there ever was one; our cat Scamp, less good-natured; and occasional frogs, newts, and other captured pets who were so single-mindedly bent on escape we soon gave up on them.

Another quick bossing anecdote comes to me when I think of some of the danger zones on the farm. One was the old chicken house the grownups finally tore down. We boys were warned more than once not to play near the untidy piles of lumber because of the danger of stepping on a nail. Mom and Dad repeated the warning I had already heard more than once: "Alec, you're just going to have to learn the hard way." With embarrassment I must admit that—try as I might to claim this characterization as unfair—the truth of it has been borne out by the facts more than once. With respect to rusty nails, I stepped on no less than seven as a boy. Fortunately, Doc Eastman was on hand after the first incident to stick me with a needle—ouch!—and vaccinate me against tetanus. Just to be on the safe side, however, Gram would have me lie down to rest each time I punctured my foot, and then she would apply a hunk of salt pork to the bottom of said foot to "suck out the poison."

Gram and Gramp, Mom and Dad, visiting aunts and uncles, and even neighbors could be our bosses at any time because, in the '50s, this was one of the many rights of being a grownup. Just about any adult could boss any kid. And if we did not toe the line, we soon heard that time-honored phrase "mind your elders." We were also instructed that "children should be seen and not heard," especially when we wanted to get our shovel in during a conversation between the grownups. Apparently, formal occasions like Christmas and Thanksgiving were especially sacrosanct in this regard. As the pint-sized members of any such gathering, my brothers and any cousins in attendance were banished

"You're Not the Boss of Me!"

to the "children's table" and instructed to "keep the noise down to a dull roar."

To keep us out of mischief generally (and to contribute to the family's livelihood), we were almost constantly employed. We stacked firewood, filled the woodbox in the kitchen during the winter, made our beds, washed and wiped dishes, shucked peas, husked corn, plucked chickens, weeded the garden, picked apples, and so on. This was expected, so much a part of the world we grew up in, we never imagined our occasional protests would gain us anything more than a raised eyebrow or—if a grownup's patience was wearing thin—a lecture on laziness or where being sassy might lead. In spite of this, we loved Mom and Dad and Gram and Gramp—they were our heroes more often than not—and we had plenty of time to play.

After weeding the vegetable garden on a hot summer morning, we'd go inside for the usual soup from a can and peanut butter and jelly sandwiches. After lunch, Mom would say the words we'd been waiting for: "All right, go out and play. Just be back by supper." When we were striplings, we would head for the Little Woods, but when we grew older we graduated to the Big Woods where we built forts. Later, growing ever bigger and stronger, we pedaled our bikes down to the village of Taftsville where we might ride Jimmy Atwood's pigs in our own version of a rodeo, play baseball with the Watsons, or watch Bruce White fire off one of his two-foot-long rockets.

I *do* remember feeling liberated upon escaping menial jobs at home. What is ironic and laughable is that, soon after jumping on my bike and making myself scarce (in case my services were needed after all), I would find myself happily pitching in on chores elsewhere. Why was working for one of the neighbors fun, when doing the same thing at home was, well, not so much fun? It is another of life's mysteries. I'm not sure I have the answer, but maybe when I tell you about Elmer Bumps, you'll have ideas of your own.

❖

"You're Not the Boss of Me!"

CHAPTER 7

Elmer Bumps, the Buddha of Sugar Hill

Mildred and Elmer Bumps, golden anniversary, 1965 (from Taftsville Tales, compiled by Pearl Watson and published by The Happy Valley Homemakers, 1967).

I f I don't count family members, my first real boss was Elmer Bumps. I use the word "boss" loosely. He never actually hired me. I was hanging around the farm one afternoon, lending a hand with this and that but trying not to get in the way, and before I knew it, I was up there every day. I was twelve. Hired man,

I was, although a little short and underweight. To be honest, if a boss is someone who gives orders and is clearly above you, the word boss is not a good fit for Elmer. For me, he was more a smiling Buddha than a boss. I imagine I would have felt calm in Buddha's presence, and this was how I felt around Elmer. His was an unhurried pace. Of course, he was an old man when I knew him, but I don't think it was just age that accounted for his unhurried way. I think he linked his throttle to the rhythms of those around him, Mildred his wife, Bonnie the farm collie, his soft-mannered cows, the catfish in the watering tub, the leaves rustling in the maples along the road. Was it a kind of wisdom? I like to think so, but I don't know. Maybe I'm just a dreamer making stuff up.

Even though he had a million and six jobs to do around the farm, he always had some time to visit, and visiting with Elmer was fun. That twinkle in his eye, the chuckles we shared over his gently humorous stories—all this put him on a par with my folks as someone I could learn from. As a kid, the phrase I used to hear for people like Elmer was "salt of the earth," as in "so-and-so is the salt of the earth." It occurred to me recently that I didn't know where that saying came from. It turns out Jesus called the fishermen, shepherds, and other working stiffs the salt of the earth because, honest and virtuous, they were as precious as salt, which in those days was as scarce as hen's teeth. And so, Elmer gets his own chapter here because, in my book, he *was* an honest, virtuous man, the salt of the earth.

I found a black and white photo of him a few years ago (not the one above) and then misplaced it. I remember comparing it to the one in my memory before losing track of it, however. That one was in color; otherwise, they were identical. His neatly cut hair was pure white under his farmer's hat. Most of the farmers I knew as a boy wore the same blue-and-white striped cap, the one first adopted by engineers driving steam locomotives. Like those of his thrifty counterparts, his hat was faded from countless washings. Beneath the visor, his sky-blue eyes were as bright and keen as ever. His face, weathered from a life spent outdoors in the wind and sun, was kind. His large, liver-spotted hands could grip a cow's teats with firm gentleness or a sixteen-pound fence maul with surprising strength. He was dressed in the clothes I remembered: bib overalls of faded blue denim, a long-sleeved, blue, button-down cotton work shirt, and tall, black, rubber barn boots. If there was a nip in the air, he topped this outfit with what farmers called a "barn frock," a light, flannel-lined, denim coat with brass buttons and a soft, corduroy collar. As the golden anniversary photo of Elmer and Mildred proves, he had other clothes packed away for weddings and funerals and such, but I never saw them.

Elmer was my first real boss, and he was also my first grown-up friend. He and Mildred lived at the top of Sugar Hill just up the road from us. They had a farm with chickens, two towering, old workhorses named Danny and Mike, a beautiful collie named Bonnie, who could have been an understudy for Lassie, about twenty-five Jersey cows, and a watering tub with catfish in it. They were all a great attraction, but it was really Elmer himself who drew me in. He coached me on how to clean the mangers, feed out the hay, clean the barn gutters properly, and do all the other chores a seventh-grade apprentice with a habit of stepping on rusty nails was qualified to do.

I loved being at Elmer's farm. I don't remember how long I did chores and other work there, but I know it was long enough to make a lasting impression on me. In the spring, Elmer and I drove the Jeep up on the hillside along the pasture fences with a load of posts, tightened sagging barbed wire, and drove new posts in the ground where they were needed. His grandson Harry and I forked the winter's store of manure into a wagon and then drove out onto the fields and forked it out again so the cows would have a good crop of hay. I helped bring in that hay during the summer with Harry and his older brother Harvey. I got a few more lessons in driving when I worked for Elmer because he let me abuse the clutch on his Jeep pick-up until I could move the vehicle forward slowly and smoothly.

I started working at the farm in the winter, though. In the evenings, after supper and after my chores were done, I stuck around while he finished the milking. I'd pull up a stool and sit near enough to talk but out of the way of the cows' switching tails. We would sit, and Elmer would wait to move the milking machines to the next two cows, both of us enjoying the comfortable quiet of the barn. Sometimes Elmer talked about the old days. One night he told me about one of *his* first jobs. He drove a horse and wagon door to door in Woodstock, carried a block of ice suspended from a pair of tongs into each customer's kitchen, and placed it in a metal-lined wooden cabinet called an ice-box, the ancestor of the electric refrigerator. I'm sure that's where he began to develop the strength that would serve him so well as a farmer. Those blocks must have been heavy by the end of the day!

Each night, after the cows' milk had been poured into milk cans and stored in the cold spring water that ran constantly into a concrete tank in the milk house, I went home, but not before Elmer filled my own half-gallon, galvanized pail to bring to Mom and Dad and my brothers. I still remember the end of my first week working for Elmer. It was Friday night, and he had just topped off my pail. I was about to leave, but he told me to wait just a minute. He pulled a worn, shiny leather wallet from his overalls, extracted a dollar bill, and extended his hand for me to take it.

"What's that?" I asked. He smiled as he so often did, and his blue eyes sparkled.

"That's a George Washington. If a fella works all week, he ought to get paid."

"Thank you, Elmer," I said. If I hadn't been carrying a milk pail, I would have skipped all the way down the hill to our house. I was pretty happy. I had my first real job, and my first boss was, well, he was the best boss a fella could have.

...

As I said, the old folks and the old ways rubbed off on us. I never realized how much until much later. It is so often the case. Out on the streets of childhood, life flashes by like a fast car. Sometimes it slows down enough for us to recognize the make and model, but often it's a blur. Now, when I think about Elmer and other neighbors and friends from my boyhood, I see that Mom and Dad, and Gram and Gramp were not the only stars I watched to set my course. Some stars were brighter than others, but all those other people, and all that was going on during those Eisenhower years in that dime-sized corner of Vermont shone a beam of light on the road before me.

Of all the elders I knew as a boy—other than my kin—Elmer Bumps stands out as someone who affected me deeply. Later, I came to feel the same way about another farmer, Albert Conklin. He and Elmer were both strong, kindly, hardworking men. They were quick-witted, wise, and prone to laughter. That laughter, like that of our folks, came from a deep well of humor which was good for the soul. I'm glad I had a chance to drink from that well. What is life worth if we can't laugh now and again? In that spirit, I'll share this anecdote about Elmer and his penchant for chewing tobacco.

As a youngster, I decided I must take up this habit as well. Elmer's Jersey cows ate good hay, and he supplemented that hay with grain and beet pulp. Looking at the beet pulp one day, I saw a resemblance to Elmer's Red Man Chewing Tobacco. The beet pulp had a purple cast to it which did not match the color of Red Man, but it was shaggy and the cows chewed it. I reasoned that if Mom and Dad wanted us to eat beets from our garden—which, being a finicky eater, I didn't want to do—the pulp was probably a safe substitute for Red Man. This shows the mysterious nature of psychology. All that was needed to get me to eat beets was the right motivation. I promptly wadded up a chew and placed it in my cheek. I worked it gamely and felt myself grow inches taller. I can't claim that I ever took up beet pulp as a habit, but I did feel closer to Elmer even from this one experiment.

Another tobacco memory comes to mind now that I have opened the pouch. One day Elmer and I were driving in his Jeep pick-up past Gram and Gramp's and on up through Happy Valley to the Hartland Hill Road where we turned right. We were headed to Woodstock to run an errand. It was a fine summer day, and all seemed right with the world. A quarter-mile ahead of us was a dusty, asbestos-shingled house right beside the road. This was just past where Scott "parked" our Jeep solidly against a power pole one below-freezing night in January and lost his shoes when he was thrown out the passenger door. He hiked in stocking feet to Mrs. Haschke's house to place the dreaded one a.m. phone call to Mom and Dad. A fella named Putt lived in the house we were approaching. I think he collected fees from Woodstock residents at the dump on Si Osmer's property.

I had ridden by Putt's in our Chevy more times than I could count, and you could place a winning bet on Putt's dog dueling with our car every time. He would run

Elmer Bumps, the Buddha of Sugar Hill

hellbent for the front tire on the driver's side hoping to carry away a mouthful of Detroit in his powerful jaws. It was annoying. Dad would mutter colorful phrases if Mom wasn't in the car and was torn between keeping to a straight line and swerving. His innate kindness made the swerve a sure thing, but it was always an exciting moment. Who could tell? Would this be the day the dog would misjudge timing and distance?

So, I knew Putt's dog would come after Elmer's Jeep that day, and I was curious about how this scene would play out with a different driver. To say that Elmer drove at a leisurely pace would be an understatement. A kid on a bicycle could have kept up with us on our way to Woodstock, but I didn't mind cruising lazily along. A few years later, Bill Birmingham and I would cover many a mile on the back roads around Woodstock at a similar speed. As Elmer and I moseyed up the dusty road, I noticed what I normally didn't—a single waving flower, a beady-eyed crow staring at me from a dead tree. We sat in easy silence. Was Elmer traveling another road at that moment, one that led back to his youth, that led to a world where the automobile was as yet unknown, where he drove a team of horses, not a car? Were we motoring down the road at the dignified speed of a trotting Morgan because he was born in another time and part of him was there still?

I don't know. Maybe he just rolled nonchalantly along because the Jeep was better suited to a farm road than the open road.

In any case, when we neared Putt's, he slowed down which surprised me because Dad usually sped up, hoping in vain to elude Putt's mongrel. Sure enough, the dog tore across the yard, barking and looking as mean as my hatchet-faced fifth-grade teacher, Mrs. Meanie, who made me write one hundred times on the blackboard, "I will not talk in class." Now, with Elmer shaving another few miles-per-hour off our speed, the dog was about to barrel into the side of the Jeep. I thought he might even leap through the driver's window and muckle onto Elmer with some very nasty-looking dog teeth. Then, a thought struck me. As usual when going for a drive, Elmer had some Red Man in his cheek. Had he spit lately? I didn't think so. *No, I told myself, he's saving it.* At the moment of truth, with the Jeep literally moving in slow motion, and the dog about to leap, Elmer turned his head to look out the side window at the oncoming mutt. Rats! For a split second my view was blocked! I heard a yelp, and as we moved past, I looked over my shoulder through the back window. The still-yelping dog was rolling in the road, trying to regain his feet. When he did, he ran so fast with his tail between his legs that he got ahead of himself and somersaulted caboose over coal engine back into Putt's front yard. Elmer glanced my way, grinning. A smidge of tobacco juice decorated his lip.

"You squirted him?" I asked excitedly.

"Mm-hmm" was the affirmative answer.

"Holy cow! Good shot!"

His eyes twinkled as they so often did. He settled back in his seat again, and I went back to gazing out the window in search of whatever I might have missed when traveling at the faster but still moderate speed of our '58 Chevy Fleetline.

Yes, Elmer, was a beacon for me. I was thinking of other ways he influenced me. Like many Vermonters I knew back then, he was not prone to finding fault. "What's the good of that?" he would have asked. Me, I can't say there's any good in it, but "to err is human," said Alexander Pope, so I admit to my share of fault finding. Maybe just knowing Elmer helped me do less of it than I would have otherwise. Elmer probably wasn't perfect on this score either. I can easily imagine one judgment he might have made on occasion, one made by many an old Vermonter. "That fella," Elmer might have said, "all he does is bull and jam." By that, he would have meant the man worked carelessly, too damned fast, and maybe even recklessly. It wasn't a compliment. To my knowledge, Elmer never bulled and jammed. He always kept the same steady pace, and he could work all day. He knew the world around him—the woods, the fields, the animals—and he usually knew the steps of the work well ahead. He did not waste steps, and he did not rush. He was in harmony with his work and his world. Now, as I approach the age he was when I knew him, I still aspire to that kind of harmony.

 I'll end this chapter with a poem I wrote in Elmer's honor years ago. Almost all of the sidehill farms like the one described in the poem are gone. The old farmers like Elmer have gone to greener pastures, but they left a surprisingly strong legacy. A new Vermont has found new ways to farm, new ways to care for the land. Some of the new farmers and land stewards are from old Vermont families and some are from "away." All that matters is that they love the woods and fields and revere the past where people like Elmer moved at a slower pace. Like the old-timers, they believe in thoughtfulness, hard work, kindness, self-reliance, resourcefulness, and thrift. Because they live in a "brave new world," they also believe in small carbon footprints, post-chemical organic farming, and community co-operation. I am grateful for this small band of new Vermonters trying to preserve the natural beauty of a place I have always called home, a place I hope will be home to many Vermonters yet to come. It's a world that may not be slow anymore, but maybe what was best about that world can still guide us.

Where I Come From

Windsor County, Vermont—1962

On their knees,

the cows stretch their long necks forward.

They strain against the stanchions,

rattle the chains anchored in the concrete.

Their tongues rasp against the manger

and curl around every last bit of silage.

When their measure of grain is gone,

they get back on their feet.

"These are Jerseys," he says

and pushes his cap back.

"You can always tell a Jersey

by the white ring around its muzzle."

I am ten and this is one of the first things

he teaches me

Cap Pistols, Cardboard Sleds & Seven Rusty Nails

The compressor kicks on and he pushes

through the whitewashed swinging door of the milkroom,

a milking machine in each hand.

The cows wait for the hay. Their tails twitch.

They shift from foot to foot. Hooves scatter sawdust.

Some are thirsty and push their noses into their water bowls.

Valves open. Cold water flows from a spring in the hill.

Iron pipes shiver and clank on the whitewashed walls.

The bowls fill. The cows drink.

The old man hooks up the milking machines.

The compressor pulls on the air in the lines, pauses

and repeats this cycle over and over, *sshhhhh—sshhhhh—sshhhhh*.

Soothing and quiet. Each grab of vacuum

brings milk into the stainless-steel pail.

A young cow kicks and a suction cup falls off, gulps air noisily,

but the old man puts it right back on.

A cow bellows and others soon take up the call.

They want their hay. I climb to the loft.

The rungs of the ladder are honey-colored

Elmer Bumps, the Buddha of Sugar Hill

and polished by all the men and boys before me.

I hook my fingers in the twine,

heave the bales and throw them down.

I break them open and feed them out.

The cows chew steadily, turning the cud over and over.

The hay soothes them at milking time.

They are not greedy for it as they are for the grain and corn.

I chew on a stalk of orchard grass while I work.

Sitting on his milking stool,

stripping out the milk the machine can't get,

he tells me a story about a man who catches a fish.

Under the brim of his hat, his merry blue eyes

and mischievous grin seem part of his story.

I don't even realize he has made it up

until the fish gets too big to believe.

Then we laugh at the whopping lie he has told.

Tilly's kittens come from their hiding places

and lap up milk from a pan I've set out

in the middle of the barn floor.

I grain the work horses, Danny and Mike.

They nuzzle me for a carrot and I stay clear of their feet.

The pattern becomes as familiar as the path

I follow through the field each day to the farm.

I can see him still, farmer's stoop, full white hair,

kindly, and still strong even at seventy-four.

His clothes are worn, but the holes are patched.

He puts on a clean shirt and overalls every day.

Every night, after I feed out the hay, the old man talks to me.

He tells me what it was like to be an orphan growing up.

He tells me about a friend of my grandfather's named Jack Baker,

about how catfish keep a watering tub clean.

He tells me things I need to know

about where I come from and who I really am.

Now, many years later, I have children of my own.

He died long ago, and I rarely visit the valley where I grew up,

where I helped work his sidehill farm.

Elmer Bumps, the Buddha of Sugar Hill

But when I smell the sweet, green scent of new mown grass,

I feel the heft of a hay bale again

and hear the cows rustling in the stable.

I see the old man sitting on a three-legged stool.

The dim light from a naked bulb shines over the walk.

He has his shoulder and face against a cow's flank

as he strips the last of her milk.

And then the vision wavers like a hayfield shimmering

in the heat of an August afternoon,

and the world I once knew disappears.

CHAPTER 8

The Horrible Three

Don't take me literally on this one. My brothers and I were not all that horrible most days. It's just that The Horrible Three popped into my mind when I was asked what we did as boys to entertain ourselves in the 1950s and '60s, but I'll explain the Horribles later. What did we do for amusement? Let's start from the beginning when we were very little Horribles looking for fun, adventure, and excitement in a world that was pretty much brand new—at least, to us.

Right off the bat, you should know we played outside. A lot. I don't know if Mom pushed us out the door, or if we ran out in a blur hoping to escape a last-second brainstorm on her part as to what new household task we could perform, a task likely to involve cleanliness and a healthy dose of monotony, scrubbing the toilet, for instance, or vacuuming our bedrooms. Once out of sight, it was an unwritten rule that we were safe from press gangs and too far away to hear Mom calling us back for one more chore. With

From left, Scott, Duncan, and Alec. It is a cool fall day, and as soon as the shutter clicks, we will hightail it into the woods.

Spike, known to Dad as our faithful "wonder dog," we would pause briefly to consider our options.

In the early days, when we still lived at Gram and Gramps' house, the options were numerous. We could head up to the hay barn, jump from high places to low places with hay to cushion our fall, and we could build forts using hay bales. We could also explore the second story of the woodshed which held many interesting relics from the days when the Harveys still ran the farm. Or, we could wander aimlessly until struck by the lightning bolt of inspiration. While waiting for the lightning bolt, we often resorted to tried-and-true

Scott with the bigger, more impressive tricycle. Alec with the sorry-looking, anemic trike. Note the chicken house which would soon become a pile of rubble where Alec would later step on rusty nails. In the fall, Dad and Gramp hung about twenty slaughtered chickens from horizontal two-by-fours on the old barn foundation and dressed them out. Mom and Gram hot-plunged them, and we boys helped pluck them. Meat in the freezer kept us going through the winter.

routines. Scott was the leader in our world of play and often cast the die that decided our immediate fate. He might, for instance, jump aboard his trike and tool around the yard which would signal us to follow on foot or look for conveyances of our own. I remember his tricycle clearly as being bigger and better than mine, and this brings us to the serpent in the garden of Eden, to the apple, and to the temptation to be less than one's best self.

This is as good a time as any to mention the cardinal rule for younger brothers back then. Take the offered hand-me-downs and don't complain. And how could any younger brother back then complain? Our parents' logic was irrefutable: "Your older brother has outgrown his Sunday school sports coat, so you need to wear it now because it's still a perfectly good jacket, and "we're not made of money, you know." Or this: "Your older brother has outgrown his bike. His knees bump his chest when he pedals. You take his. We'll find a bigger one for him." So, the older brother gets a new (I'll admit, probably used) bike that is bigger and altogether more impressive, and you get his rust-speckled, dented, but "still perfectly good" bike. You know you're too small to ride the bigger bike, but you still want to ride it. You want to ride it badly.

Ah, temptation rears its ugly head and hisses. I confess here that I'm not only talking about younger brothers in general, but also about yours truly. I admit also to adding another episode to my already long list of what I had to "learn the hard way." When Scott got his much taller, blue Columbia bicycle, I *begged* to ride it. No doubt, somebody gave me permission just so they wouldn't have to listen to me beg until the cows came home, until the cockerel crowed the break of day, until—well, you get the idea. I promptly dumped it, drove a handlebar into my stomach, and lay gasping on the ground like the fish we often pulled out of Happy Valley Brook.

One of us, I think Duncan, had a pedal-powered metal car you could actually sit in and drive if you pushed wicked hard on those pedals and stayed on more-or-less smooth, flat ground. When we began watching T.V. westerns, we often rode broomstick horses around the yard. Dad, seeing our sorry nags one afternoon on arriving home from work, found time at school to jigsaw and paint some horsehead profiles from one-inch pine, glue a pole into a neck-hole on each one, and bring each of us a new, trusty steed to ride instead of a ridiculous broomstick. We galloped around the yard with new enthusiasm, our mounts whinnying, the pole gripped dangerously between our legs, reins held firmly, yelling, "Yippee-ai-tai-yay!" and "Hi-yoh Silver!" praying silently, God don't let me trip and cause pain in my unmentionables. We were inspired to play cowboys and Indians by *Gunsmoke, Rawhide, The Rifleman, Cheyenne, Sugarfoot,* and other

Duncan in car, Scott on the too-small truck, and yours truly on the trike.

westerns which aired on prime-time television after dinner. *The Lone Ranger*, starring Clayton Moore as the masked hero and Jay Silverheels as his Indian sidekick Tonto, we watched every afternoon.

Now that I think about it, television inspired a lot of our play. We loved toy guns of all kinds, plastic squirt guns, plastic tommy guns, metal Colt revolvers, cap pistols, and pop guns. If we could imagine a *bang* and a whistling bullet, we were in heaven. The N.R.A. had nothing on us. Dad made Scott a wooden facsimile of a rifle in the school shop. It was clearly a muzzleloader with a cocking mechanism he could pretend to pull back for firing. It was cool! Our cap pistols were an especially exciting novelty. We bought them at J.J. Newberry's department store in White River Junction, or maybe they arrived with our cowboy outfits at Christmas. J.J. Newberry's had a couple aisles devoted to merchandise for kids. It was our favorite toy emporium, and we always went there to shop before Christmas. Only J.W. Barber's store in West Leb could compete with Newberry's, mainly because Barber's carried coveted army surplus items like canteens and mess kits and camp axes.

Ah, but don't let me forget the cap pistol. How did one fire a cap pistol? You stuck a red, dotted paper roll into a compartment in the gun and fed the end through a slot in the top of the pistol. Every time you pulled the trigger, each dot of black powder encased in the paper would move into position, the hammer would fall, and—*bang!* The gun would actually fire! It was lots of fun to squirt each other with squirt guns, especially on a hot day in July, but once we discovered cap pistols, the squirters were set aside. Much later, we were allowed to own BB guns. They shot little round balls about an eighth of an inch in diameter. Of course, the advent of BB guns was accompanied by our first lessons in gun safety, and the by-now-familiar but imperfectly grasped concept of responsibility once again made an appearance in our developing minds.

When Dad taught us to shoot real guns, his first admonition was this: "A gun is not a toy." Of course, we didn't want to disappoint Dad, so we did our best to act grown-up as we learned about the safe use of firearms. He owned two 0.22 caliber Remington rifles and a Stevens of the same caliber. One of the Remingtons was a single-shot, and the other had a clip and could be fired multiple times without reloading. Something about the way Dad approached the whole thing really made an impression. Maybe it had to do with the way he and Gramp had already laid the groundwork. Dad had told us stories about his boyhood for years, and these included brief mentions of squirrel hunting with a twenty-two when he was a lad growing up in West Leb.

And then there was the often silent but larger-than-life figure of Gramp. Every November, just before Thanksgiving, he would appear in red-and-black wool pants and coat to head off up the hill in search of the wily buck. For me, this ritual vested him with an air

From left, Mom, her sister Bev, Gram Shattler, Duncan (already the young Scot), and Dad. Unknown person at extreme right holding spotting binoculars. Looks like somebody just fired from the shooting bench. Note the sand bag on the mini-jack being used as a shooting rest. I hope those aren't whiskey glasses on the table!

of mystery and linked him to the past. We had heard stories about Hastings marksmen who won turkey shoots in the old days, and I saw that Gramp was one in a long line of hunters. Yes, the groundwork was laid. In fact, it was so well laid, Scott shot a buck by the time he was twelve. I can see it now in my mind's eye, hanging in the woodshed for a few days, curing, until it was time to butcher it. Venison! Free meat! It raised Scot's stature in the family.

Dad's stories and Gramp's example acquainted us with their attitudes about guns long before we ever touched one. Then that day came, the day we pulled the trigger. Dad took us to the rifle range, the sand bank in our yard that had still not been landscaped after our house excavation. There he taught us gun safety and marksmanship. After warning us never to point a gun at anyone, to always remove the cartridges when not in use, etc., he had us set up paper targets. After he gave us tips on using the open sight, raising the barrel slowly, and squeezing the trigger lightly, it was quite exciting to see the bullet holes in the target move closer and closer to the bull's eye as our aim improved. When we were allowed a little more leeway, I remember setting up my three-inch high, plastic, World War II infantrymen on that sand bank and knocking them over.

All this talk of guns, and cap guns in particular, reminds me of another discovery we made. We decided to experiment with the rolls of cap-gun ammunition in new, inventive ways. Some finely-tuned instinct prompted us to move a discreet distance away from the house. We left the backyard and set up shop on the stonewall that marked the boundary between Gramp's land and the Bumps'. We wondered what would happen if we exploded the caps by hand. I can't explain why we were so entertained by tapping and popping the caps with small stones. Boys and small explosions? Maybe today it would come under the heading of "creative play." Anyway, it was while we were using the stonewall for cap popping that we noticed garnets. We were prone to close inspection of the natural world. Watching ants work for the first time was good for several minutes of intense concentration. A blue jay feather found in the Little Woods, a woodchuck skull found in the field, or a vacated paper wasps' nest? These were objects of fascination, treasures we contemplated for days. For a long time, I had an orange crate display case full of such items in the bedroom Duncan and I shared.

When we saw the garnets—small, metallic gray, faceted stones embedded in shale—we chipped away at them carefully and released them from their prisons. We collected them in small bags and became "wealthy dealers in gemstones." When I say "chipped carefully," I'm sorry to say we did not use safety glasses. Once again, some angel of mercy must have been looking over our shoulders. I'm not sure if our discovery of the garnets kick-started our prospecting and amateur geology careers, or if it was our discovery of gold.

That discovery came through our love affair with water. Before we were old enough to go alone to Happy Valley Brook to swim or fish, we explored puddles in the yard, the frog pond in the old brickyard, and the stream that divided the hayfield halfway between our place and Gram and Gramps' house. This small tributary of Happy Valley Brook had cut through the till over the centuries to a depth of four or five feet. We called it The Gully, and it was a favorite place to play. One day, moving downstream from the path that connected our home to Gram and Gramp's, we got down on our haunches for a closer inspection. Maybe we were hunting frogs or newts or water skippers—we had the predatory instincts of Neanderthals—or maybe we just wanted to get wet, I don't know. As with so many great discoveries, this one was made by chance. A ray of sun slid down into the tiny pool at just the right angle. Looking down through a few inches of clear water, we saw glinting, yellow specks on the mud bottom. Gold! Could it be? Holy mackerel! We were rich! Dad could quit teaching shop at Hartford High! He could stop being an assistant principal which, by the way, seemed to be the principal cause of recurring headaches. We

The Horrible Three

could buy Mom a mixer for the kitchen or maybe even a new vacuum cleaner!

You can imagine our faces, the vanishing smiles and the dashed hopes, when Mom broke the news to us gently. "That's not real gold. It's called pyrite, also known as fools' gold." I saw the faintest trace of a smile come and go like one of the trout in Happy Valley Brook when she said that last part. Oh well. At least she didn't have the heart to scold us for getting our clothes all wet and muddy.

One other adventure in geology is worth mentioning. Across the fence, in the same pasture where we so often visited the frog pond, was the site of an old brick-making operation. Apparently, there was excellent clay in that pasture, and hundreds of bricks were baked there and used in building houses in Woodstock and other nearby towns. I remember a woman stopping by once, and digging some blue clay out of the bank so she could use it to throw pots. She said it was beautiful stuff, very pure.

We explored the site of the long-forgotten brickyard from one year to the next, and as the pencil marks Mom made to mark our height climbed higher on the door casing between the kitchen and living room, we finally turned our attention one fine day in June to the gigantic culvert that drained the pasture

The Spaulding Brickyard was long gone by the time we moved to Happy Valley, but we could still find plenty of leftover bricks sticking up out of the grass near the frog pond where we so often played. The Vale of Snares where David Balfour tracked the Horribles is at the top of the hill in the background behind the roof peak (photo courtesy of the Woodstock Historical Society).

---

of spring run-off and summer downpours. It was three feet in diameter, just big enough for small boys to pass through on their hands and knees without a full-on attack of claustrophobia. By the time we were ready to brave this passage on that summer morning, only a trickle of water flowed in the bottom of the pipe. Making our way through the slimy tunnel to the

The Horrible Three

light at the other end, we encountered our own Lost World, one no less fabulous than the one Sir Arthur Conan Doyle described. Peering out from the end of the culvert we gazed down on, not just a gully, but a ravine. Or no, not just a ravine, but a canyon! Below the pipe, the ground dropped away at an alarmingly steep angle. A silvery thread of water splashed in the shadows far below. We looked downstream into the dimly lit distance and saw that both sides of the ravine rose up at the same treacherous, almost unclimbable angle and were anchored only by the roots of hemlock trees.

Boys and climbing go hand in hand. We clambered around to the righthand bank of the ravine, clinging to tree branches and seeking even the dinkiest footholds in which to wedge our sneakers. Then, we made our way, inch by perilous inch, toward the top where bank swallows lived and where Warren Bumps' cabin had once stood in a clearing until he sawed it in half and dragged it away with his bulldozer. The slope we were climbing was so steep and so shaded, it had little vegetation other than trees and a few ferns. Reaching out for the next tree root and hoping it would hold, one of us—Dunc I think—made the last great, rockhound find of our childhood. It was a smooth, symmetrical stone protruding from the clay. He pulled it out. It was as round as a spoon on one end and came to a spear point on the other. We found more of these odd stones. They were of all shapes, some elliptical, some amorphous, some as round as a silver dollar, but all were of the same, smooth, hardened clay. Years later I learned they were concretions like those found in Button Bay on Lake Champlain. A concretion forms when clay platelets are carried downstream to a place where the current comes to a standstill. Then, the platelets drift lazily down through the water and "cement" with others of their kind to form an object like the ones we found in the Lost World. What a surprise it was to learn years later the explanation for the existence of the concretions in our backyard. During the retreat of an ice age, a glacier dropped gravel and other debris, damming the Connecticut River and turning it and its tributaries into Lake Hitchcock. Happy Valley had once been under water!

•••

When it rained or the weather was otherwise just too miserable, or when we needed rest, we didn't have video games, but we did have board games like Uncle Wiggly and Candyland, and later, Monopoly, checkers, chess, parchesi, and cribbage. We watched serialized T.V. shows like *The Lone Ranger* and *Superman* almost daily. One of my favorites was *The Early Show*, which aired reruns of movies just after suppertime. Many of these films were set during World War II because, of course, the war had ended recently in 1945. For some reason, the 1949 movie *Twelve O'Clock High* popped into my mind. I mentioned it to my wife Denise, and she said a cousin of hers named Paul Comi acted in the T.V. series spawned by the film in the mid-sixties.

We also read a million comic books and regular books, and as I mentioned in "How the Hastings Boys Became Bookworms," one of our favorite series featured a character named Freddy the Pig. This brings us back, finally to the title of this chapter, The Horrible Three. Once again, I've used poetic license. It wasn't actually the Horrible Three, it was the Horrible Ten. We first encountered the Horribles in *Freddy the Cowboy*. They were a band of rabbits who came to Freddy's defense, and Scott decided to use the name when he and Jimmy Watson formed their first clandestine club. One day, while on patrol in the cellar, trying to track Scott's movements, I noticed a cardboard sign over the door of the fallout shelter Dad had built during the Cold War. One word was written in capitals at the top of the sign: HORRIBLES. Below that was written **KEEP OUT**. The sign also included a drawing of a skull-and-crossbones and a dagger dripping blood. Obviously, Scott and Jim meant business. The age of secret societies had begun.

Scott would say little—actually nothing—about the business of the Horribles. No self-respecting member of a secret society would ever reveal its secrets. This made Dick Watson and I all the more determined to find out what they were up to. One of the main tasks of a secret club was to have a secret clubhouse or fort, a place where secret club business could be conducted without the pesky interference of younger brothers and their friends. The fallout shelter must have seemed like a good start on an impregnable fort. It had one, easily-defended door, and Mom and Dad had stockpiled enough water jugs, canned vegetables, bottles of ketchup, spam, and other supplies to last for months.

Unfortunately, neither Scott nor Jimmy could remain on watch all the time, and they rightly suspected that Dick and I were trespassing on club property in their absence and "messing around with their stuff." That led to at least a couple years of undercover fort building in The Little Woods, The Big Woods, and other more secure and heretofore unknown locations. My most memorable encounter with The Horribles

The Horrible Three

took place on the hill above Elmer Bumps' farm. This was almost entirely new territory at the time. I had only been there once to help Elmer fix fence.

All of us younger brothers were in league in our efforts to track Scott and Jimmy's movements. For Dick and me, surveillance of the Horribles was a favorite pastime. One day, however, when I was the only watchman on duty, I saw them head up over the hill behind the Bumps' farm. I was nervous about following them—who knew what they might do if they caught me—but I felt it was my duty to spy. I waited until they were out of sight, told Spike to stay home, and then stalked them across hill and dale, feeling like David Balfour on the bonnie braes of wild heather in Stevenson's *Kidnapped* (another of Dad's favorite books). I passed from the lower hayfields into an upper heifer pasture and drew closer and closer to the sugarbush for which Sugar Hill was named. As I neared the top, I entered a small vale where saplings had grown up just shy of the bigger trees at the boundary of the pasture and the forest. I followed a well-trodden path, stepping around cow flaps, and I found myself under the boughs of trees. It was autumn, and fallen leaves covered the ground.

I felt a strange quiet descend on the glade. It was a warm afternoon. The birds napped, and the air did not stir. A preternatural awareness came over me. I stopped and studied my surroundings, looking for any sign of Scott or Jimmy. They were nowhere to be seen. Then, something caught my attention, but I was unsure of what it was. Slowly, I swung my head through the same half-circle, staring. There it was. Ten feet away, a sapling bowed down to the ground. And then I saw another. They were ahead of me along either side of the path. It was mystifying. Why would these trees be bent over that way? Perhaps winter snows had weighed them down so badly they hadn't sprung back. I approached the nearest one carefully. Something looked wrong about the leaves on the trail where the crown of the tree nearly touched the ground. I swept a few aside.

There beneath the leaves, a loop of rope had been cleverly hidden. Scattering more leaves, I saw that it held the treetop. It had been set to snag anyone walking that path. If the loop was pulled, it would trigger the snare, and the stout sapling would yank the victim off his feet and into the air. I took a stick and tested the trap. Holy hot dog! The young tree whipped up into the air like a catapult, strong enough to take a young heifer off its feet. Yep. The Horribles meant business. For all I know, Scott and Jim were sitting in a forever undiscovered hideout, watching

The Horrible Three at the OTTER ST. ONGE AND THE BOOTLEGGERS book launch party, 2013.

the whole incident through binoculars and smirking at the horrified expression on my face. If not, they must have still felt especially satisfied later when they learned of my close call and the breathless account of the adventure I shared with Duncan on my return home.

I could go on and on about our pastimes, our forts and toys, and our endless invented games. I haven't even mentioned our winter activities. Oh, when I think of our sled races, our ice climbing adventures, our— well, I can only say winter deserves its own chapter. Yes, I could go on, but who of us has the time to hear so many snippets of story? Only children have such riches before them, and isn't that as it should be? Let the children have their magical world. Let them have their adventures and their hairbreadth escapes and their eternity of time. Such things are all part of growing up. And let all who might feel sorry for the children called baby boomers—the generation born soon after America's G.I.s returned home after World War II and married their sweethearts, the poor kids who didn't have video games or cell phones—let all who might feel sorry for them be comforted. For the baby boomers of Happy Valley, there was never a dull moment, and I imagine the same was true for bunches of boomers everywhere.

◆

The Horrible Three

CHAPTER 9

The Snowsuit

When I reached middle age, I drove out of the village of Taftsville one day and up the Low Road to my boyhood home. It was a fine fall day and the leaves, gold and orange and red, flamed in the sun. I had children of my own by then, and—as the old folks used to say—"a lot of water had passed under the bridge." Suddenly, I came out from under the leaf-dappled shade along the brook and into the bright sunlight of Happy Valley. I felt a quickening in my heart. I pulled off onto the verge and rolled down my window. Perched on the hill above me was the home Dad had built for us decades before. It looked as it always had. Then, I considered the hill itself, the one that had once loomed as large as a Swiss alp. What had been Mt. Everest in my imagination, I now saw for what it was, a mere nubbin of a hill. How was this possible? How could my poor excuse for a memory have exaggerated so? I stared at the hill nonplussed and was visited by wistful thoughts about the mirage of childhood.

But other thoughts slipped in uninvited and soothed me. I squinted against the light, and these thoughts magically transformed themselves into shapes, two figures near the crest of the hill. *How strange*, I thought, *they are so far away.* It was as if the hill had become a mountain again. I saw Scott and Duncan up there, huffing and puffing, dragging our old toboggan that last bit of the way to the top. A wind rose, and snow whirled up and blew away like a genie escaping from a lamp. My brothers reached the trail they had already packed by making several runs. Scott spun the toboggan around with the rope and pointed it toward the bottom of the hill. He and Dunc plunked down, ready for the next ride. I stared up at them. Did Duncan just wave? Then, I heard Scott's voice. Even coming to me from far, far up the hill, it was unmistakable.

"Hurry up!"

"Yeah, hurry up!" Duncan called.

I turned off the car and opened the door. *No*, I thought. *This hill is just as big as I remembered.*

•••

When I dive down the woodchuck hole and come up in Happy Valley sixty years ago, I see Duncan staring out the picture window of our living room. He looks downcast. Has Mom told him it is too cold to go

The Snowsuit

outside today? Is he a prisoner of the arctic front that settled in two weeks ago? He has recently learned to read the outdoor thermometer, and the needle seems to be stuck on zero even though the sun is shining. Tonight, it will drop to the twenty-below neighborhood as it has for over a week. Ah… what now? He perks up. A snow devil materializes a hundred yards away and spins madly across the diamond-flecked field toward Grammy's house. Duncan follows this tendril of winter smoke with his eyes, and what is that in his expression? Disappointment because he cannot go outside to give chase? No! It is the fiery gleam of excitement because as soon as Scott and I make our beds we will all go out together.

"And how," you ask, "did pipsqueaks like the Hastings brothers withstand the bone-deep cold that would freeze the nether parts of an Eskimo?" Simple. We armored ourselves like King Arthur's knights in the best snowsuits the Sears & Roebuck catalogue had to offer. I still remember the grownup's admonition: "Bundle up, it's cold out!" They weren't fooling, as we soon found out when we lost a mitten or got snow down our boots. Fortunately, Mom didn't throw us into the deep-end right away. Long before winter arrived, she had been working to protect us from the grip of Jack Frost. By November she and Gram had knit the last pair of two-color mittens, the last stripy socks, and the last wool hat. Snowsuits had been patched and handed down, and, yes, maybe a new one had arrived from Sears. Then, we waited.

Every morning we gazed at the sky and debated whether the clouds moving over Happy Valley held snow or more disappointment. We listened to weatherman Marty Engstrom on Mt. Washington for news of a blizzard. Day after day, nothing happened. Then, when we were about to give up hope, we woke up one morning a few weeks before Christmas to find a foot and a half of snow on the ground and the flakes still falling. Winter was officially launched! Only one job stood between us and the great outdoors—bundling up. This task required our full attention, which was a challenge for me because my mind tended to wander. It could take half an hour to bundle up, more if you put the cart before the horse. You could not, for instance, put on your boots before your snowsuit.

"Crud!" I said the first time I did.

"Watch yourself, mister," said Mom, "or you'll get your mouth washed out with soap." I muttered and kicked my boots off in Scott's direction because he was smirking. This may come as a shock to the parents of well-behaved children, but while we were in our *Lord of the Flies* stage, Scott and I declared war on each

The Snowsuit

other. Our weapons—teasing, a covert punch on the shoulder, the theft of comic books, and occasional knock-down-drag-outs—were *de rigeur* for a number of years. We were reminded from time to time that we were brothers and should learn to get along. We would try for a while, but a chance remark would blow the lid off the powder keg, and hostilities would resume.

Many years later, when it was already long established in my mind that our prickly relationship spanned our entire boyhood, I had the chance to paw through the bin of family photos Duncan inherited after the folks passed away. To my surprise, there were quite a few photos of Scott and me together, black and white snapshots taken before Mom began to tire, when she still bathed in the proud glow of her two, cute boys. The ones where we stood side by side in our Christmas cowboy suits, our swimsuits, our going-to-Sunday-school suits didn't convince me we were pals. We had enough respect for Mom and the sake of posterity to stand still for the few seconds it took to hear the click of the Kodak. On the other hand, there were a number of candid photos that showed Scott and me playing—together! Clearly, they were not staged.

One of them stands out for me. It's the one where we are riding tricycles in the yard at Gram and Gramp's, and the old chicken house is visible in the background.

Scott is pulling a wagon loaded with sticks. It is a picture of two boys going happily about their business of learning the use of the wheel. It was yet another bit of evidence that the memory is not entirely to be trusted. Maybe Scott and Alec's War did not span the entirety of their youth, but maybe peace broke out now and again. It also reminded me of how narrow my vision has been in times past when I could see only the road in front of me and not the hills and valleys through which it passed. I was probably in my thirties when the teachings of psychology had gained enough of a foothold in the public's awareness for the idea of sibling rivalry to filter down to me.

"Sibling rivalry? Explain it to me again, please," I said to Deb, my lovely second wife.

"When a second child is born, the first child can feel abandoned and resentful. For instance, if we are talking about boys, the older boy can feel angry with the second child who he sees as an interloper. This helpless being who can't walk, can't say a single word, this nuisance who only cries and makes a mess in his diaper, *this* child is now the center of attention."

Hmm. I thought about this and filed it away. I thought about it again when I saw that photo. I also thought of that night at Camp Billings when headlights flashed through the window of our attic bedroom, and

The Snowsuit

I got out of bed just in time to see Mom and Dad's car driving away. I was afraid they were abandoning me, and panic overwhelmed me. So maybe Scott felt abandoned? *Nah, not Scott.* Hmm. Then again, how would I know? Maybe. So much of life is a mystery as it flies by.

•••

But this isn't getting us out the door and into the arms of Old Man Winter. If you remember, I had just kicked my boots off, slyly aiming them in Scott's direction under the table. This went unnoticed. Mom had stepped out of the kitchen, and as Duncan walked by, Scott grabbed his scarf.

"Hey, let go!"

"You went into my room last night and took one of my comic books, didn't you?"

"I did not!" cried Duncan indignantly. This was true. *I* had taken the comic book. It was hidden that moment in my closet. I made a mental note to return it as soon as possible.

"Right. I bet."

"What are you boys doing? You better not be fighting!" Scott tugged on the scarf, grabbed the sleeve of Duncan's snowsuit, pulled him off balance and sent him sprawling on the kitchen floor. Duncan scrambled to his feet, and I could see by the look in his eye that all hell was about to break loose. Shrill music rent the air, urgent notes every soldier heeds. Duncan mouth-bugled the U.S. Fifth Cavalry's call for a charge! Scott and I knew this call well from the television series *Boots and Saddles*. We also knew that in two seconds Duncan would grab the nearest object he could find and peg it at his tormentor with all his might. What made both Scott and me run for cover on these occasions was the knowledge that, in the heat of the moment, it didn't matter what that object was. It could be as light and small as a salt shaker or as big and heavy as one of our metal kitchen chairs. Scott was already heading for the living room. Sure enough, Duncan grabbed one of my boots and threw it like Red Sox pitcher Bill Monbouquette. It nailed Scott in the back of the head and landed on the floor with a thud.

I don't want to give the wrong impression here. Duncan's name means "brown warrior," but our younger brother was more of a peacemaker than a troublemaker. Nevertheless, he sometimes found himself between a rock and a hard place when Scott and I tried, simultaneously, to recruit him for missions into enemy territory. Sometimes he got caught in the crossfire when our skirmishes erupted. Then—watch out!

The Snowsuit

"I told you boys you'd better not be fighting!"

"We're not, Mom!" called Scott.

"Scott Oliver!"

"Okay, Alec threw a boot at me, but he missed. I thought he took one of my comic books." By this time, Mom had reappeared in the doorway to the kitchen."

"Enough! Get dressed and go out! I'm not putting up with any more of this horseplay. Be good!"

"Sorry, Mom!" we echoed. Shaking her head, Mom went back to cleaning the tub in the bathroom. The bathtub seemed to need a *lot* of cleaning. How did three boys attract so much dirt even in the winter? It was another mystery whose solution escaped me, and I had no time to ponder it given the tense atmosphere in the kitchen. Duncan sat down in the chair Scott had just vacated. There was more muttering.

"Move," commanded Scott in a low voice. "I was sitting there." Duncan stuck out his tongue, but he shuffled stiffly over to the door in his new snowsuit. Somehow, he had managed to get all his duds on ahead of Scott and me. I headed for the bathroom.

"Mom?"

"What?" she said with an exasperated sigh.

"I gotta go." I don't know why, but "having to go" was just one of those things that happened sometimes as soon as you put on your snowsuit. By the time I got back to the kitchen, Scott was stomping around in his school boots. He couldn't find his deer hunting boots, so he had to wear his black galoshes with the buckles. These were good for school days because they went on over your shoes. After you stomped around a few times, your shoe would go all the way in, and then you could fasten the four buckles to tighten the boot. They were good enough boots, I guess, but deer hunting boots that showed off your red-topped wool socks had a lot more cachet. Maybe this was why Scott suddenly grabbed my hat off my head and winged it down the hall.

"Mom, Scott took my hat!" I yelled as Scott ducked out the door.

...

I wanted to duck out that door myself, but I had one more thing to do. Being a hand-me-down, my snowsuit was broken in, and I could move faster than Duncan. I galumphed up the stairs to my bedroom, retrieved Scott's comic book, and slipped it into his stack hoping, but not really believing, he would think he hadn't noticed it during his check of inventory. Then, I dashed downstairs and out the door.

Splat! A hard-packed snowball hit me in the head.

"That's for stealing my comic book." I turned. Scott

Scott with new ammunition. Alec on the run!

was scooping up more snow, molding another missile, and almost ready to fire away. I saw our toboggan by the swing set and ran. A second snowball whistled by my ear. Suddenly, I was back in the war. I put on a burst of speed, grabbed the pull-rope, and headed for the hill across the road. I was soon out of range and slowed to a trot.

At the top of the hill, I stopped and looked down. The prospect of a high-speed run down the face was exciting but not without problems in need of a solution. Who, for instance, would sit at the front of the toboggan? The answer was obvious. Duncan. Scott and I both knew that the guy in front got a face full of snow, especially on a first run in deep powder. Duncan knew this, but it had been a year since he had sailed down the hill for the first time in a rooster tail of snow and had to roll off at the bottom and scrape off the cold, wet snow that was plastered to his face. He was the youngest. Maybe he had forgotten by now how cold that snow was. Probably not. What cunning plan could I devise that would convince him the front of the toboggan was the seat of honor?

I must admit to feeling a little ashamed of thinking this way. It was ironic that Duncan, the youngest, had a moral compass that showed true north most of the time. Oh, he might wander off a few degrees now and then—every compass has a magnetic declination—but he was generally a good kid who did the right thing. Scott and I, on the other hand, hardened by years of warfare, had become a little devious. When I checked my moral compass, it read south, east, or west as often as north, and I suspect Scott's was the same. Still, moral ambiguity had its advantages. Duncan now stood at my side eyeing the steep slope.

"Are you going down?"

"'Course." Scott appeared, laid the rope down

The Snowsuit

the length of the toboggan, and positioned it for the launch.

"Let's go," he said. "Dunc, you can have the front." Just like that, Scott solved the problem. Scott shoved off, and the three of us sped down that hill yelling with delight, all our past battles and future stratagems forgotten in the thrill of the moment. We spent a couple hours sliding down that hill. The track became well packed, and each trip was a little faster than the one before. Just before lunch Dunc surprised us.

"I wanna go down by myself." Scott and I looked at him doubtfully. The toboggan run at our feet was daunting and he was only six.

"By yourself?" I asked.

"Yeah."

"You sure?" asked Scott.

"'Course." I had a feeling like grit in my shoe, a tad uncomfortable but not especially noticeable. A quiet voice in me said one word. No. But what could go wrong? The track was steep, and now it was twice as fast as when we started, but we always coasted to a stop on the long flat stretch before reaching the road. Scott and I exchanged glances and then shrugged.

"Okay," we said in unison. Duncan sat in the front of the toboggan and gripped the top where the wood had been steamed and bent into a curl. Pulling up on one side or the other would allow him to turn left or right or—if he tugged too hard—flip the thing completely over. I gave him a push and he moved off slowly down the first few yards at the crest. Then, he picked up speed. A swirling cloud of snow veiled the toboggan as it rocketed down and down, faster and faster. He was flying, just one, lightweight little kid on a mission worthy of a fighter pilot. Then, Duncan burst out of the cloud at the bottom and sailed across the flat heading for the road.

"What the heck!" said Scott.

"Uh-oh," was my only reply.

He was going so fast the toboggan barely touched the snow. I looked up and down the Low Road. Thank the Lord—no car in sight. Not many went by back then, but you didn't want to count on that. Si's honey wagon could be coming up out of the woods, or John Doten might be taking another pass with the town plow about then. Duncan reached the end of the track and *continued* across the snowy field like a runaway train with ten boxcars pushing him from behind.

"Bail out! Bail out!" we yelled from the top of the hill. He couldn't hear us. He dashed across the road holding onto the toboggan like one of the

The Snowsuit

Fifth Cavalry being chased by Apaches. Then, he disappeared as jets of snow burst in the air all around him. We waited, straining our eyes to see. Slowly, the snowflakes sifted down and revealed a scary, scary sight. A limp silhouette hung from the barbed wire fence that ran down that side of the road. It was our younger brother, looking like a snowsuit pinned to a clothesline. We ran down the hill in the track, breaking through, stumbling, falling, and finally reaching him. He looked stunned, and his face had been scratched. He was otherwise, miraculously, unhurt. He had, indeed, been "clotheslined" by the fence. Being closer to the ground, the toboggan had shot out from under him and continued down toward the brook leaving him hanging. I believe to this day that it was that brand new, stiff-as-a-board, Sears & Roebuck snowsuit that saved him. Scott carefully separated the fence barbs from that suit while I went after the toboggan. The three of us trudged up the hill, sobered by the whole experience.

"Might be better not to mention this to Mom," said Scott. Duncan nodded his head, still shell-shocked.

"She'll see the holes in the snowsuit," I said.

"We can say we saw a deer heading to the brook, and Dunc got tangled in the fence when we went down to look."

"Good thinking. But what about his face?"

"I don't know. You can figure that one out."

"One of the snowballs we threw had some dirt in it."

"Who threw it?"

"We're not sure." We looked at Dunc. He nodded glumly. Once again, my moral compass went south. Oh well, it was bound to read true someday. When we got back to the house, Mom called us in for lunch. She had Campbell's tomato soup and—oh joy!—peanut butter and marshmallow sandwiches waiting. We struggled out of our snowsuits. Hoping to postpone an interrogation about the rips in the new suit, Scott and I piled ours on top of Dunc's while Mom was busy at the stove.

"How was the tobogganing?"

"Good!" Scott and I answered a little too enthusiastically. Mom looked more closely at Duncan.

"Any problems?" This question was clearly directed at our younger brother.

"Nope," he piped up cheerfully. "It was great. I had one run where I went so fast..."

"You went so fast you had to bail out, didn't you?" said Scott with a barely detectable note of warning in his voice.

The Snowsuit

From left, Duncan, Alec, and Scott. Snowsuits were also good for just sitting in your snow fort and sucking on an icicle.

"Yeah," said Dunc, chastened. "It was really great, Mom." And he went back to slurping his soup. As I said he was a good kid, but wandering a few degrees off north—well, now and again it's the best course. Thank goodness he caught on quickly. Sometimes, mum's the word.

❖

CHAPTER 10

Newton's Law in Winter

"When an apple falls from a tree, it must keep rolling lest it freeze."
(NEWTON'S FIRST LAW OF MOTION IN VERMONT)

It is widely believed that the Yankee work ethic originated with the Puritans. In fact, it was a response to the weather Vermonters describe in this phrase: "nine months of winter and three months of darned tough sledding." Let me explain. On almost every winter day in the Eisenhower and Kennedy years, Vermont mothers reached a point when they were fed up with their sons' rambunctious behavior. This usually happened soon after breakfast. How did they cope? They translated Newton's first law into language boys could understand, saying simply, "It's time to go out and play!"

"Mom, I just barely finished breakfast!"

"I don't care. You and your brothers get your snowsuits. And don't talk back."

"But it's cold! It's zero!"

"You'll live."

Resigned and secretly excited about what new adventures awaited us outside, we donned our hats, coats, snowpants, boots, scarves, and mittens. We tumbled out the door and found ways to "live" that would have made Darwin proud. Although we did not know of Newton at the time, we gravitated toward him instinctively. Motion! That was the answer to survival. Preferably "loco" or crazy motion. This, then, was the real reason the work ethic took root in New England. Winter taught everyone the only way to stay warm was to keep moving!

Our early experiments with wintertime locomotion did not show great imagination. Familiar as we were with the wheel from our summertime use of the tricycle and the bicycle, we tried to figure out how we could get some fun out of the wheel in winter. We did have one success. One morning the snow was especially good for making snowballs. The snowball was guaranteed fun day after day. We could usually run around for an hour or so, yelling, "Attack! Attack!" or "Retreat! Retreat!" firing snowballs from the parapet of a snow fort, setting ambushes, and so on, until somebody took a hard hit or until our mittens got soaked and our fingers went numb.

Anyway, this one morning we stumbled on

something new, something that harked back to the invention of the wheel. This story may even shed light on how the wheel was really invented. We had crossed the road to the top of the hill where Duncan had made his famous solo toboggan run, the one where he had shot across the road and into the fence. I don't know who started rolling a snowball. It's like asking who invented fire or the arrowhead. No historian was present, and the inventor's identity is buried in the sands of time. But it took shape before our eyes, something new. It wasn't just some measly snowball that we would have used for a snowman's bottom or his big round stomach. No, this was bigger, and the snow was just right. It wasn't falling apart.

We kept rolling it across the top of the hill, and by the time we finished, it was taking all three of us to push it. Finally, it got so big we could barely move it. We coaxed it to that point where Newton could take over, where gravity would lend a hand. It moved slowly at first, like Duncan pushing off toward glory that other day. It picked up speed, and by this time it was rolling up all the snow in its path. There were stalks of grass sticking to it. It was no longer a ball. It was a gigantic jellyroll of snow, and now it was going so fast it was bouncing slightly and taking little skips. It became a juggernaut. Near the bottom it was flying, and when it hit a bump, it went airborne. I can't quite describe the satisfaction we felt when it landed. Of course, it didn't explode like fireworks that fly off in all directions. It was snow. Heavy. Slumpy. But somehow the splattering of that tractor-sized snow wheel sent little sparks of happiness through us.

I can only compare the feeling to our discovery of tree-tipping in later years. One day we happened on a dead tree in the woods. We studied it. And then— an idea came unbidden. I don't know who made this discovery. Again, the sands of time blow across the wastelands of memory. It doesn't matter. Let's say it was our trail-blazing older brother Scott and his friend Jim Watson. One of them laid hands on the tree and pushed tentatively. Nothing. Then, getting serious, they both leaned hard into the tree, looking at the top a little anxiously as the tree teetered. Would that wood-peckered piece break off and tumble down on their heads? The tree was teetering, but it wasn't falling. What to do? They couldn't walk away. They pushed harder, grunting, straining. Then, it came. That satisfying crack. The tree moved ponderously, and like the giant snowball obeying Newton's law, it gained speed. It took down branches from a neighboring tree and landed with a thunderous crash that shook the ground. Alarmed crows rose *caw-cawing* into the air and flew away. Duncan and I learned of this earthshaking event, of course, and carried out experiments of our own. For years afterward the Hastings brothers and their friends would pause before any deceased tree in the woods, consider angles and risk, and then lean in and hope for a tip.

...

But back to winter. As I said, our early experiments with locomotion were tame. Then, one day we made the discovery that would change winter forever—sledding! Discovery? You, reader, are disappointed now, perhaps. Everyone knows about sledding or sliding as it was also called. Why do I refer to it as a *discovery?* Ah—think back, way back. There was a time when *you* didn't know about sliding. And then, one Christmas morning, you found a large, oddly shaped present leaning against the wall behind a tree festooned with colored lights and shiny balls and thin strands of foil like silver hair. The present was swathed in wrapping paper, a whole roll.

"Can I open it now?" you asked.

"Yes, go ahead."

And from the folds of paper came the most beautiful thing you'd ever seen, like Venus rising from the waves. It was a sled. In my case, it was a Champion sled with red racing stripes on the thin wooden slats fastened to the light steel frame and runners. No doubt, it was Scott's sled first, but I must have inherited it, because I remember riding it to glory many times. Oh boy, do I remember. Speed! Forget the jellyroll snowball, forget tree tipping, forget snowball fights. This was excitement!

I am amazed at what Mom and Dad allowed us to do back then. These sleds were only practical for use on a snow-covered road. Granted, there were very few cars on our road, but still, there were some. What were they thinking? We began learning how to slide on the small hill in front of our house. The best conditions were right after a snowfall when the road had been plowed but not sanded. One lay down on one's stomach with this type of sled and scanned the road ahead from an eye level eight inches off the ground. We quickly mastered the steering, swooping back and forth by pulling on either side of the handle that flexed the runners left or right.

I mention my amazement at being allowed to slide on those roads partly because Duncan and I remembered an especially close call. He was sliding down that very hill, practicing his skills when he met the milk truck. Neither of us is sure of exactly what happened, but I seem to remember that he survived only by shooting under that big-wheeled vehicle. Was Elmer's son Warren (a.k.a. Bumpy) driving the milk truck? Did he stop by to chat with the folks about Duncan's derring-do? It's entirely possible, but who knows? Painful memories are often long lasting, but maybe this event was so scary Duncan blocked out the details.

I'm not sure if any parental rules were imposed after this close call. I think Scott and I had been sliding for a few years by this time anyway. It was a mile from the top of the hill at Elmer Bumps' farm to Watson's Country Store in the village. This became a favorite run for us and the Taftsville kids. Scott, Duncan, and I would pull our sleds up the short hill to Elmer's and then stand at the top and catch our breath. Ahead of us was a mile of the fastest, most exciting sliding in the world—or at least in our corner of Woodstock. I remember seeing Olympic bobsledding years later and thinking, *heck, we did that*. Well, not really. But when you're a kid, hills are mountains and sleds are rockets.

We never dawdled long at the top of the hill by Elmer's because the prospect before us was too exciting to hang around. Eventually, we developed the technique of pouncing on our sleds so our weight and forward motion would give us a jackrabbit start. Off we went. We gained enough speed going down the first hill to coast handily across a flat stretch. After that, the road dropped down and down and down, and soon we were going faster than we had ever gone before, faster than we'd ever gone on our bikes, faster than on our toboggan, almost as fast as we went in our dreams. The trees flashed past, and we were racing.

That rang the bell on the carnival high-striker. Racing! I was in the lead. I glanced over my shoulder, and Scott was coming up fast on my left, almost within reach. I turned my attention back to the road. Good thing. I was too close to the snowbank. Suddenly, my sled lurched to the right, lifted, and buried itself in the snow bank. Scott had ditched me! I hurtled onward like a little circus man shot from a cannon. Seconds later, shaking the cobwebs out of my brain, I picked myself up from the snow angel I had involuntarily made. I looked down the hill. Duncan and Scott were dropping out of sight where the High Road pitched down yet again.

I leaped on my sled and gave chase even though Newton's law told me I had no hope of catching them. Soon, I was fifty yards behind, but I still couldn't help what I felt—a flood of exhilaration. The road rushing at me, the blinding speed! I was suddenly one with my sled even if it was now the "Not-Champion" with the red racing stripes. I reached the fork below Mr. Nichols' house where the Low Road came in on my right and joined the High Road. I looked down past Mr. Parkhurst's house and saw no cars coming up the hill, so I hugged the left. I glanced right as I reached the fork. Just my luck! A car was barreling toward me down the Low Road from Happy Valley. Should I ditch again or could I make it? I gripped the steering bar and prayed. I whizzed through the fork ahead of the car, shifted back to the right side of the road, blazed past the Morgans' house and the Patches', and then crossed the bridge over Happy Valley Brook.

It was the same bridge where, in another race, someone had again given my sled runner a yank. That time, I slid sideways, looked out through the space under the bottom rail, saw my death waiting, and swerved away. I pulled off the road below the bridge and went back to look, quivering. The track of my sled runner was inches from the edge. If I hadn't recovered, I would have plunged fifteen feet straight down into the icy, rocky brook. Heavens to Murgatroyd!

But I'm sorry for jumping out of the story. That first day, racing Scott and Duncan, I didn't stop. I cruised down past the Howes' and the Dietrichs' and swept into the yard of the old school, where I pulled in behind a snowbank and hid. I heard the car go by, the one I had darted out in front of at the fork, the one whose driver was probably still muttering, "Darn kids." I stood up, grabbed my rope, and pulled my sled behind me past the Burnhams', the Whites', past Smack and Elnora Watson's farmhouse, and arrived finally at the store. Scott and Duncan were sitting on the green bench to one side of the door, eating candy bars, drinking sodas, and looking a little smug.

"Where have you been?" asked Scott.

"Wait till next time," I said. He just grinned.

"Boy, you hit that snowbank like a sack of potatoes!" said Dunc. "Are you all right?"

"I'm fine. Is Dick here?"

"He and Jim are getting dressed. We're going back up to Elmer's." said Dunc.

"Good." I went inside to get a Tootsie Roll and an Orange Crush. The day's racing was not over. Victory was still within reach. Or defeat. Either way, it was going to be fun.

...

Before I close this chapter, I have to mention a couple other pastimes. For me, the Champion sled and the Speedway pinned the winter fun meter day after day, winter after winter, but we also had exciting— sometimes hair-raising—adventures on the Watsons'

The Taftsville Store. The Watsons, Hastings, Whites, and other kids in the village played football and softball on the lawn to the left of the store (photo by Johnathan Schectman, 1997, courtesy of the Division of Vermont Historic Preservation). Harvey was a pretty good sport about the occasional broken window.

traverse, on wooden skis, and even on cardboard. Scott and Duncan remember the Watsons' traverse as one of the big ones that would carry eight or ten pint-sized kids. It was so big it would accommodate all the older Burnham kids, and that was no mean feat. The Burnhams' large family moved into the village halfway through my boyhood. Now and then, I visited Bimbo, who introduced me to a favorite Burnham pastime—the Ouija Board.

Anyway, the Burnhams, who numbered more than the birds in the sky, were welcome on our traverse excursions because that old sled weighed a ton. A horse would have been a big help in pulling it to the top of whatever hill we decided to conquer. Boy, that rig must have been at least ten feet long, and it was solid. As Dad would have said, "It took two men and a boy to pull it." In our case, it took a contingent of original Taftsville kids beefed up by the newly-arrived Burnhams. Once at the top, all complaining was replaced by a tense excitement. With ten kids on board, Jim Watson, the helmsman, had a heavy responsibility. It took a minute or two for Newton's law to kick in. The traverse getting under way was like a train leaving the station. It lumbered along at first, but then it built up steam. We bubbled with excitement like a teapot about to whistle.

"Holy smokes! This is going to be a lightning run!"

"Yeah, look how fast we're moving already!"

"A little to the left, Jim. You're takin' her too wide."

This tip was from Jimmy Atwood, who was scared of frogs but was apparently an expert on avoiding traverse crack-ups. Jim ignored him. He had the T-bar firmly in hand and was guiding us smoothly through the shallow bends of the High Road. There were no sharp corners on that road. It just went down and down like a falling arrow. That was a good thing because the traverse wasn't a sled you wanted to be on when it was sliding sideways in a curve, especially when some joker was steering who decided to pull the T-bar hard for a quick steering correction. Such a stunt was likely to fling the whole load of riders into the tree-lined snowbank.

As the traverse gained momentum, the riders stopped talking. The only sound was the rumble of the steel-shod runners. The trees flashed by, and we broke out into the open at Mr. Nichols' house with the steep hill before us and the fork below. It was the moment of truth because trying to avoid a car at the fork with the traverse was a lot riskier than with a sled. A quick dodge left or right was impossible. In looking back, I wonder if we were partly protected not only by the small number of drivers on the road, but also by the fact that most of them knew they were likely to meet kids on sleds. Or maybe there were other forces at work in the universe, and for reasons of its own, the fickle finger of fate waved us on that day as on so many others.

•••

The last sliding story to complete this chapter's triad, concerns Dunc and me and cardboard. Scott may have been with us, but I don't think so. As time went by, he went his own way more and more often.

When Dad finished the second upstairs bedroom, he took apart the maple bunk beds he had made for us, moved them upstairs as twin beds, and Dunc and I moved in across the hall from Scott, who already had the other bedroom to himself. The orbit each of us would follow for the next few years had been set. Exactly what caused the constellation in which Scott's star traveled at a distance, and Duncan's and mine traveled in company is hard to say. Was it some primal pecking order? Our own mutable inclinations? Impulses that sprang from our mysterious hearts? I don't know. Who *can* know the past? It is a ghost we see in a mirror.

But this I *can* say with certainty. Newton's laws were at work again on the day of the cardboard sliding adventure. One of those mysterious, midwinter thaws had come, and it had even rained. The mercury dropped in the thermometer overnight, and igloos and ice fishermen were again safe. Mom and Dad had recently bought a washing machine, and as luck would have it, they had not yet thrown away the cardboard shipping box. Hallelujah! Under Mom's watchful eye—I wasn't certified for solo knife use yet—I cut the cardboard into sled-sized pieces.

Because we were now magicians at putting on our winter clothes, ten minutes later we were standing outside at the edge of the field. Our dog Spike bounded up over the snowbank left by the plow, and we followed. Then, we took that first step onto the field that would tell all. Had there been enough melting and then enough cold to form a boiler plate crust, one we could walk on? Yes! It was so hard we barely made a dent.

"Where do you want to start?" asked Dunc.

"The spring" (see cover photo—above and to right of car).

"Oh yeah, that'll be good! We'll go fast!"

We did, in fact, go fast. Newton would have been proud. The spring was situated halfway up the hill in the middle of what was a hayfield in summer. That meant we had acres of sliding which were free of trees or stone walls or other dangers. So we thought, at least. As it turned out, it took us longer than usual to get to the spring. When we reached the steep slope below it, we had to kick into the crust with our boots. Like the mountaineers we had seen on T.V. scaling peaks in the Himalayas, we had to fashion steps. Slowly and carefully, we climbed. If we slipped, we would skitter down the hill like hockey pucks.

Finally, we reached the top and plopped onto our squares of cardboard to catch our breath. Spike sat too, and we all looked down on our Happy Valley home. It looked smaller from that distance. We gazed out over the fields, now shimmering as the sun poked through a few holes in the scudding clouds. Smoke plumed from the chimney at Gram and Gramp's house. Grammy must have just put a few sticks in the cookstove. It was peaceful. But as the ancients said, "Time and tide wait for no man," and soon we felt Newton's pull. Somehow, we sensed an impending, unnameable danger. By now we had logged hours and hours of sliding, and we felt pretty sure of our racing skills, but that voice, which speaks ever so quietly and is so rarely listened to by boys, spoke now. I just couldn't make out what it was saying.

"Be careful," I said to Duncan. He must have heard the sense of foreboding in my tone.

"I will," he replied quietly.

We flung ourselves onto our cardboard squares, grabbed the leading edge in mittened hands, and took off down the hill. It was the usual sliding story, at least at the beginning. We started off slowly and gathered speed. Spike was keeping pace and barking excitedly. Then, the gathered speed began to multiply. Exponentially. Cardboard on ice! It was fast, oh yes, wicked fast! Spike's barking faded, and I realized we had left him behind. As we reached the flatter slope just above the house, I expected to slow down, but that didn't really happen. We were flying, and there was no stopping us. I worried for a second that we would soar over the snowbank and slam into the house, but the field pitched slightly to the right down toward the brook that ran through the field, and we veered off in that direction.

This was when I realized two things I should have realized before striking out on this mission, two things which now put us in peril. First, we had no way to steer these cardboard "sleds." Second, braking was going to be a problem. With a metal runner sled, you could drag your feet. It scuffed your boots badly, but in an emergency those boots could mean the difference between piling into a tree and coasting to a stop unhurt. Unfortunately, I thought dragging our boots on the hard crust that day was going to have little effect. In seconds we were going to pass from the hayfield into a triangle of land between our house, the road, and the brook. Underneath the snow in that part of the field, a section unmown in the summer, was marshy ground tufted with hummocks. It never froze as solidly as the field above because of its sponginess and its crop of dead swamp grass and goldenrod stalks. The sun coming out had allowed us to kick into the crust while climbing the hill, but it wasn't easy. All this flashed through my mind as we sped toward disaster.

I didn't like the idea of careening into that pocky patch where the crust might thin out and break like brittle china.

"Bail out! Bail out!" I yelled. This cry rang out in the valley whenever a crack-up was in the works. I took my own advice and rolled off the cardboard. I pinwheeled away, my snowsuit as good a sled as my cardboard. But pounding with my mittens and kicking hard with my boots, I finally slowed down and came to rest against one of those hummocks at the edge of the marshy no-man's land. Duncan zipped by, holding on to the cardboard for dear life, a captain staying with his ship. He entered that wild triangle and a terrible thing happened. He broke through! Spike caught up with us, barking in a frenzy. I scrambled across the icy crust to help. Dunc didn't move. He lay face down. *Oh boy,* I thought, *this isn't good.*

Just as I arrived, he jerked as if somebody was trying to start his engine. Then, slowly and painfully, he rose from the snow. He had gone through the crust face first. Blood was streaming off his chin.

"Can you walk?" He didn't answer. He just shuffled toward the house. I think Mom might have screamed when we came into the kitchen where she was making lunch. I mention this because Mom wasn't given to screaming. Maybe it was just a yelp.

Anyway, she was shocked. She quickly ushered Duncan into the bathroom and administered first aid. Scott appeared.

"What the heck happened to Dunc?"

"Huh?"

"I saw you guys walking back to the house."

"Had a little accident." He shook his head.

And so closes the chapter on the great, untelevised Happy Valley Sled Races of the 1950s and 60s. We not only absorbed our work ethic then—we worked hard at sledding!—we also learned a lot about Newton's laws in winter. Kinetic energy keeps you warm, speed multiplies force, and when an apple falls, no one knows where it will land.

CHAPTER 11

The Great, Silent Cal State Park Vacation

Mom and Dad were new to vacationing when Scott and Duncan and I were kids. Back then, the idea of a vacation was still unfamiliar to most Vermonters. Like many of our neighbors, we came from farming stock, and of course, farmers have cows to milk, endless chores to do, and little time for "frivolous" pursuits. Even though our grandparents no longer farmed, old habits die hard, and I don't think our parents heard much about vacations as kids, especially since they grew up during the Great Depression. Probably, the closest they got to a vacation was a Sunday picnic, a trip to the grandparents, or a reunion with relatives at a wedding or funeral.

Whoa! Hold up. As the pictures below prove, I am an unreliable narrator. Gram and Gramp *did* go on real vacations at least twice. She and Gramp went to Florida with her sister Annie and Annie's husband,

Ernest Marchetti. In my defense, I don't think Gram and Gramp ever went on a vacation until after World War II. Until then, they didn't have the extra dough. Their other vacation was a trip to Europe, a reward from the Twin State Fruit Corporation for Gramp being the top beer salesman one year. Included in the itinerary was a visit to Italy, the home of Gram's parents, Santino and Adele Fontana. *"Favoloso!"* as my great grandparents might have said.

Gram sunbathes on a beach in Miami.

The Great, Silent Cal State Park Vacation

Both these vacations are evidence that Gram and Gramp—along with many other Americans—joined what would become known as the Affluent Society. In that America, people did have extra money! Soldiers returning from the war built new houses, put newly-invented fiberglass insulation in the attic and walls, installed triple-track aluminum storm windows, and paid for oil-fired furnaces to carry heat to every room.

Gramp Hastings, Ernest Marchetti, and the Florida parrots they befriended.

Lord love a duck! Suddenly, the average Joe and Jean had landed in the lap of luxury! Along with these improvements came the forty-hour week, and that most enticing invention, the weekend! Before long, people were enjoying week-long, company-approved vacations! Mom and Dad must have been excited about the prospect of "a vacation," but as we boys were soon to find out, they didn't know a lot about how one might actually commit a vacation... or conduct a vacation... or just go on vacation. Vacations were so new, people didn't even know exactly how to talk about them!

They were eager to learn, however. First, one had to have a destination. Perhaps, having an inkling of what it was like to travel with three boys for any distance, Mom and Dad made a wise decision on this score. They chose Calvin Coolidge State Park as the site of our first family vacation. The campground was only twenty miles from our home in Taftsville. As close as it was, it might as well have been on the other side of the moon, but more about that in a moment. Once they chose a destination, Dad and Mom had to prepare. That short, two-syllable word does not really communicate the scale of this enormous undertaking. How, for instance, would we travel to our destination? What would we eat, and where would we stay?

THE GREAT, SILENT CAL STATE PARK VACATION

Our blurry, maroon Classic with the Monkey Wards roof rack ready for Dad's cartop carrier. I have no idea how the Rambler happened to be parked in front of this imposing stone building.

Obviously the challenge before us was real, but we took heart in knowing that George Marshall had rebuilt Europe after WWII. If he could succeed in that massive task, we could get survive a journey to the wild western edge of Windsor County.

Fortunately, this was the golden age of the automobile. Dad was entirely confident that we could drive to Silent Cal's Park in our four-door Rambler Classic with its chrome-plated trim.

This was also the golden age of the campground and the motor hotel (later shortened to motel). Since we were relatively low on the Affluent Society totem pole, Mom and Dad opted for a campground, and the problem of accommodation was solved. Hurray! We would drive to Plymouth, Vermont and camp like cowboys and Indians for an entire weekend! Pesky questions kept popping up, however. Where would we sleep, and what would we sleep in. What would we sleep on? How would we cook? Thanking their lucky stars, Mom and Dad remembered the two-inch thick, mail-order catalogues they often used for doorstops or booster seats at the Thanksgiving table. Sears and Monkey Wards sent these wish books out several times a year. How many fantasies they must have spawned for those who thumbed through their pages. They were to the '50s and '60s what Amazon.com would become in the early twenty-first century. Mom and Dad began ordering right away: a family tent, sleeping bags, air mattresses, a camp stove, a camp lantern, and so on.

Packages began arriving daily, and Mom and Dad surveyed the mountain of gear growing higher and higher in a corner of the Hastings Highland House office. We all suddenly realized that camping takes a lot of gear. Gear! *Ge-e-e-ear!* Just saying the word makes

The Great, Silent Cal State Park Vacation

me salivate even now. When you're a boy, gear means a jackknife or a hatchet or a compass or some other amazing tool that will help you survive in the woods. For Mom and Dad, the immediate problem was where to *put* the gear. We were all proud of our new Rambler Classic, but the trunk would hold little more than an ice chest, a tent, and a camp stove.

And if the trunk was packed to bursting, and we boys were sandwiched between sleeping bags and pillows and whatnot in the backseat, where would we find still-needed storage space? The roof! As always, Dad came to the rescue with yet another woodworking project—the car-top carrier. He had ordered our first roof rack from Monkey Wards, and he commenced building the plywood box he would attach to that rack. As he assembled the box, we wondered about its stout construction. When I think of it now, I am reminded of the pram he built, the boat we used on Knapp Pond in Reading where Mom and Dad bought a piece of land and hoped—as part of another vacation scheme—to build a camp. The pram, with its famous "frat (flat) front," was well put together with brass screws, marine-grade plywood, and knot-free planks. He painted the hull a dark green, and the inside a lovely shade of light blue. The pram provided the family with some good times on the pond—once a crew of us managed to get it on the water. It was hefty.

This was also true of the cartop carrier. As with everything Dad built, he built it to last. By this, I mean that he built it a little heavier than it really needed to be—just to be safe. Once he slapped a couple coats of gray paint on it, it was time to muscle it up onto the rack. I don't know how he got that monster up there, but he did. He tightened the nuts on the bolts to secure the box to the metal bars, and then we boys ferried the last of the gear from the house to the car. Finally, Dad ran a rope through the eyelets of the oiled canvas cover, through the eyebolts on the side of the box, and the job was done. Somewhere, I knew Calvin Coolidge was waiting with a healthy measure of excitement and a dab of uneasiness. The Hastings family was headed his way!

So, the day finally came. I'm not sure what the weather forecast was, but it didn't matter what weatherman Stewart Hall said on WCAX-TV because forecasts were even less dependable in the 1950s and 60s than they are today—way less. Given what was to happen later, I suspect there may have been mention of a shower in the forecast. Nevertheless, I have no doubt that we all left Happy Valley in high

The Great, Silent Cal State Park Vacation

Scott, Duncan, and I agreed that the Silent Cal vacation trip took place during a deluge of biblical scale, but this picture of Duncan and Scott sitting in the sun on top of a fireplace built in the 1930s by the Civilian Conservation Corps shows the tendency of memory to exaggerate.

spirits, excited about camping and sampling this exotic experience called "a vacation."

I also have no doubt that the high point of the trip occurred somewhere between our departure from our Happy Valley home and our arrival at Watsons' Country Store ten minutes later where we stopped for a small wheel of Crowley's cheese and some saltines we could snack on that night by way of celebration. If we were running true to form, the three of us boys were fighting in the backseat by the time we pulled away from the store and headed west on U.S. Route 4. We quieted down when Mom and Dad threatened us with going to bed early—that was unthinkable with the prospect of a campfire—but then Scott jabbed me with an elbow, and I "accidentally" stomped on his foot, and we were off and running again. Ours was a cold war at the best of times and a flaming hot one at the worst. I suspect Duncan had the unenviable task of sitting between us before we had driven many miles down the road.

Our cries of, "He hit me!" and, "You hit me first!" must have made the trip seem longer than it was, especially for Mom and Dad. Making the journey even longer would have been the pit stops where Duncan or I would dash into the woods to "see a dog about a tree" (because we had refused "to go" before leaving home), a stop for Dad to check the roof rack and the tires, a stop for Mom to check the map, and an occasional back-tracking maneuver when we got lost. The road to Plymouth was paved, but it followed the winding Ottauquechee River, and before long I was as green as a Martian. Dad stopped, and I opened the door just in time to upchuck on the gravel of a picnic pull-off instead of on the Rambler's upholstery. For this, all were grateful. Duncan and I both got queasy whenever we encountered a road with twists and

The Great, Silent Cal State Park Vacation

turns or swoopy sections, and of course, this included almost every road in Vermont. Mom usually had a paper bag handy in case Dad couldn't pull over in time, but we never liked to admit we needed one, so there had been "accidents." All these delays served to make a half-day odyssey out of a trip that would normally take an hour.

I asked Scott and Duncan what they remembered of this vacation, and Duncan, not surprisingly, remembered details Scott and I did not. I think he is like our father in this way. Dad had a particularly good memory. Duncan remembered our brand-new, green sleeping bags, our new family camping tent, and our new Sears camp stove. Scott remembered our camping lantern and its mantles (little net bags) that captured the outflowing gas and glowed brightly when lit—at least until one of us kids bumped this technologically advanced marvel. The mantles were delicate and fell apart easily if jarred. If a mantle fell apart, we boys listened carefully hoping to learn new profanity from Dad if Mom was out of earshot.

What we all remembered was the rain. I think God may have given us just enough time to set up the tent before it began to pour, but he certainly didn't give us time to build an ark or make other preparations that would have saved us the misery so many early

Scott and Duncan are resting. Maybe they look content because Mom and Dad have finally ceded victory to the rain, taken down the tent, and our departure for home is imminent. Duncan is smoking the campfire cigarette mentioned below.

---

car campers suffered when they discovered that the manufacturers from whom they bought their tents and clothing made over-enthusiastic use of the word waterproof. There may have been lulls in the rain, I suppose. Shown photos (included above), I grudgingly acknowledged this. Duncan remembers having a campfire during one of those lulls. He said he remembered us smoking cigarette sticks.

"Do you mean those candy cigarettes we used to buy?" I asked.

"No, I mean real sticks. We got them burning and then pulled them out of the fire and put them in our mouths. They kept smoking for a bit, and we pretended they were cigarettes." We were used to seeing Gramp Hastings smoke, so this made us feel grown-up.

But the cigarette sticks were a short-lived amusement. The rain fell for hours and hours, and gradually spirits dampened right along with everything else. The "waterproof" tent sort of worked—for a while. Then, it gave up and began to leak. That led to wet sleeping bags, then wet clothes, and then the dawning realization that we were living in a bathtub, and the tub was filling up. By the end of our exotic vacation everything was wet. More than wet. Sopping wet. Soggy. I suspect we adjourned that adventure a little early. I don't remember ever using that cartop carrier again, not for camping anyway.

The Silent Cal Vacation Trip was not the end of our efforts to commit a whopper of a vacation, however. Before long, Mom and Dad purchased an Apache pop-up camper, and we took a position a little higher on the Affluent Society totem pole. Mom and Dad also bought that brush-choked, mosquito-infested piece of land down on Knapp

Pond where they hoped to build a stout but humble cottage, one with a waterproof roof. But these are stories for another time. It is enough to remember for now that the Great Silent Cal Camping Trip—exotic as it was—was just a stepping stone to even more spectacular vacations. In a world where Neil Armstrong was about to step foot on the moon, we had high hopes that great adventures lay ahead.

❖

THE GREAT, SILENT CAL STATE PARK VACATION

CHAPTER 12

The Undiscovered Country

In 1965 I was fourteen and about to become a freshman at Woodstock Union High School. Scott was sixteen and beginning his junior year. At twelve, Duncan still had a couple years left at the elementary school. We were growing up. Great Gram Lena Belle Hastings had passed on in 1963. Cuttings from her Christmas cactus still grow in Hastings homes. Great Gramp Oliver joined her a year later. We visited him at an old folks' home across the river in Haverhill, New Hampshire not long before he died. We couldn't go inside, so Dad took us across the lawn to his window. We were only about eight feet apart and could see each other clearly through the glass. He smiled broadly when he saw us. I will never forget how happy and how sad I felt on seeing him there, happy because of his obvious joy at seeing us and sad because I sensed he would be leaving us soon.

Spike, our constant four-legged companion, had made the journey to those Elysian Fields where dogs happily chase woodchucks from morning till night.

Scamp, our circumspect cat, lingered in a shadow world. I imagine him hiding out in Happy Valley to this day, peering from behind a screen of grasses or stretched out comfortably on the branch of a tree looking down on unsuspecting passersby. We packed the magic of our Happy Valley childhood carefully away in the attic with our sleds and stepped tentatively onto the stage of adolescence.

Boyhood was now receding in the rearview mirror, and manhood stood somewhere on the road ahead with his thumb out. But what signposts marked that stretch of highway as we drove into the undiscovered country of our teenage years looking for the men we hoped to be? We all have different milestones, but in my remembrance of this time our experiences with girls overshadow all other memories. Why? Because girls were on the other side of that equation called love, and every young man wants to find X. It was my bad luck to flunk algebra. I pined for girls mightily during high school and fell off the cliff of love time after time. Most guys would have found a lesson in so much failure. I just kept falling. Girls were like mermaids. I took great joy in their beauty, but I could never catch one. Always when I got close, they vanished like a dream on waking. I knew the girl I was looking for was in a town somewhere in that undiscovered country, but just when I thought I was getting close, a flagman would send me down a backroad detour to Nowheresville, or I'd get a flat tire, or—you get the picture. The delays were endless. And the worst of it? I had a feeling my manhood was in that same town.

But in spite of my impatience, the days passed as steadily as the beat of a metronome. The smell of change was in the air like the first whiff of spring. By the summer of 1965, Mom had been working in Woodstock for a few years, and the Hastings brothers were still riding with Ken Barrup to Woodstock every day to go to school. One day Mom dropped the bombshell.

"Boys, your father and I have talked it over. We are thinking of moving to town." We shouldn't have been surprised, but we were. We were *quite* surprised. Happy Valley was, after all, home. We knew no other, could imagine no other. We had questions. Of course, Mom had answers.

"You're all making new friends at school, and if we move to town, you'll be able to see them more often. Alec, you're always wanting to visit Freddy Doubleday and Bill Birmingham. Scott, you're always on the go with Jimmy Roberts and Rick Harding. Duncan you'll be in the same boat soon." This was true. We nodded but were not exactly excited. "And with you in

Fred Doubleday with hat and older brother David (circa 1970s). The best of friends.

My lifelong friend, Bill Birmingham.

---

track, Scott, and you in basketball next year, Alec—well, we make a lot of trips to town. Scott, you'll have your license soon. Dad and I are not thrilled about you driving up over Hartland Hill during mud season or a snowstorm. It's getting to be too much." We couldn't argue with any of Mom's points. This was beginning to sound like a decision that had already been made, but what could we say? The logic was ironclad.

Then, the same question occurred to all of us.

"What about Gram and Gramp? Will they be moving too?"

"We'll see. We're looking at a house with an apartment, and we're hoping they'll live upstairs."

Mom felt all three of us would have more opportunities if we moved to the village. We would see our friends more often, play sports, go to school dances, use the library to study (and see girls), and we could even find jobs. We *might* have experiences we couldn't even imagine yet. All this turned out the way she pictured it. We did those things, even some we never imagined.

The move was good for Mom, too. If she invited new friends to dinner, they no longer had to brave our dirt road in one of those snowstorms she mentioned. In town, friends were minutes away. If she needed groceries, she could drive to Ray Houghton's Red & White store faster than we could say high, diddle, diddle. She could walk to work. She could see people daily. Yes—the move was good for us and for Mom. I don't think it affected Dad much one way or the other. As it turned out, he was to drive to his job in White River Junction for another five years, and it didn't matter whether he left from Taftsville or Woodstock. I imagine he saw the sense in moving, however. The only real question in his mind must have been the same one we raised. What about Gram and Gramp?

Did Gramp want to move? I doubt it very much, but I never talked to him about it. He loved the farm. It must have been tough for him to give up the woods and hills of Happy Valley and move into the apartment above Mom and Dad. After the move, his outdoor life was limited to mowing a postage-stamp lawn and cultivating flower beds, but he made the best of it. He was proud of his old-fashioned hollyhocks and his carefully tended backyard. Did he miss the farm? I imagine he did, but he wasn't one to complain. He moved for Gram's sake, I'm sure. He was still working for Twin State, still selling to customers up and down the Connecticut River Valley, and he must have realized how lonely she would be. She had never learned to drive, so she would have been stuck there in not-so-Happy Valley. Not many women her age did learn to drive. Cars weren't common until the mid 1920s, and by then she was a mother. So, she was always home, and without her grandsons stopping by, well yes, she would have been lonely.

I was sad about moving, too, but maybe sadder in looking back than I was at the time. It seems like such a loss now, that beautiful piece of land. But who of us brothers would have kept it, could have kept it? How would we have paid the taxes? I loved Happy Valley. We all did, but farming was going out, and taxes were going up. Maybe the move was just in the cards for us. Gram and Gramp sold the old place just before the great wave of people from "away" washed over Vermont.

Once Romaine Tenney's Ascutney farm was plowed under for Interstate 91, once our Hastings cousins' farm in Grantham, New Hampshire was steamrolled by Interstate 89, once all the small farms in the way were bulldozed, the denizens of the Eastern Seaboard were able to zoom northward on the new super highways in a few hours. As Dad would have said, "they came in droves," eager to escape the sardine life of the city. They were weighed down with coin they wanted to spend, and they loved the quaintness of Vermont and Vermonters, the cows plodding along well-worn paths on green hillsides, the small villages of neatly kept colonial homes, and the overall aura of an idyllic, vanishing way of life. They bought run-down farms like penny candy. Once they shelled out the market price in '65, Ed and Dona Strauss became the lucky new owners of Happy Valley Farm. She taught math at Dartmouth College and he taught anthropology at the newly opened Canaan College. A few years later, they sold the old place to Laurance Rockefeller's resort corporation for about twice what they paid Gram and Gramp.

And so, we moved, Gram and Gramp moved, and it seemed as if everybody was moving. In looking back,

The Undiscovered Country

I wonder what the neighbors thought the first time they heard the wild music of the pipes coming from our backyard at 3 Golf Avenue. Maybe they thought *we* came from "away." Maybe George Williamson, the Scot who managed the Woodstock Country Club, clinked his whiskey glass with Georgina's and said, "Bottoms up, luv. Here's to the Highlands." Maybe the heavily rouged, octogenarian cat lady across from Gibby Wood's house on the corner wondered if someone was strangling one of her sixteen felines.

And then there was the Woodstock-worthy plaque Dad mounted by the door of our one-up, one-down apartment house. Many of Woodstock's elite proudly displayed a date of construction on a fancy plaque by the front door of their stately homes on The Green, Elm Street, and River Street. Visitors couldn't help but be impressed on entering a Greek Revival house built in 1820 or 1836. There weren't any such plaques on Golf Avenue before we arrived, so what was the story behind the sign Dad hand-lettered so beautifully? Who could have built a house in Woodstock in 1066? Did Scott Hastings believe Vikings had settled in America before the Pilgrims? Only history lovers would have known the Battle of Hastings was fought that year, and that was the key to the mystery. Dad was a Hastings, the house presented a remodeling battle; *ipso facto*, it was the Battle of Hastings. And of course, he was pulling the leg of any Woodstockian who liked to put on airs.

Moving into town was a big change for us, but it was dwarfed by changes in the world around us. We brothers understood by then that Dad's fallout shelter was not quite as peculiar an idea as we had once thought. Three years earlier, a U-2 pilot had flown over communist Cuba and spotted missiles capable of delivering atomic bombs to all major U.S. cities. The United States and the Union of Soviet Socialist Republics were still waging The Cold War, so the missiles rang alarm bells in Washington. President Kennedy strapped on his six-gun and met Castro in the street. "Send them back to Khrushchev or draw, pardner." Luckily, Cuba and the Russians kept their pistols holstered, but it was a tense two weeks. A year later, however, President Kennedy was assassinated. His White House was called Camelot because many people saw his presidency as one with high aspirations and chivalrous ideals. When Camelot fell, the world reeled for years afterward.

I will never forget Kennedy's death in Dallas, Texas on November 22, 1963. It happened right after lunch. I was sitting at my desk in Mr. Bean's math class that day. Duncan was in Mrs. Gaffney's room. Principal Hurley whispered briefly with Mr. Bean at the door.

The Undiscovered Country

It was clear that Doom had come. Mr. Bean couldn't hide his shock. Duncan said Mrs. Gaffney cried before she pulled herself together and sent her class home. Up at the high school, Scott went with Jim Roberts, Pete Sawyer, and Rick Harding to an assembly in the gym to hear the news. Forty years later in 2001, I was a teacher at Whitcomb High School in Bethel when terrorists flew a plane into the Twin Towers. I was in the school library and watched those skyscrapers crumble and fall on television. In sixty-nine years, that is the only other event I remember of such magnitude. It would be hard to overestimate the impact of the Kennedy assassination on the United States. It was enormous. The Vietnam War soon spun out of control, riots erupted in our cities, and divisions in America led to widespread strife and distrust. The American Dream was under siege and is still at risk today.

But life goes on, as they say, and as the sixties moved forward, life returned to normal for the Hastings brothers. Even the move to Woodstock seemed like only a pothole that made a big thump when we passed over it but was forgotten farther down the road. Being young, we lived a life tuned to the seasons not the years. Spring arrived. Scott ran the 440 and threw the javelin on the Wasps' track team. He joined the Woodstock High School Drama Club as a junior or senior and played

*Scott's high school senior picture. Brylcreem.
"A little dab'll do ya!"*

the lead in *The Dutch Detective*. He was a nattily dressed, Edwardian detective replete with spats, pin-striped suit, derby, pencil mustache, and a suave demeanor. In an earlier chapter, I mentioned Aunt Annie's comparison of Gramp to the actor Clark Gable who played that handsome devil Rhett Butler in *Gone with the Wind*. I've always thought Scott inherited Gramp's Rhett Butler charisma. He had the same, crooked Hastings' smile, and he had a glint in his eye that hinted at mischief or at being in on a joke soon to be told.

Two of his high school flames stand out in my memory. Lena was a statuesque blond.[5] I hesitate to call her exotic—she was not a creature in a zoo—but it's the word that comes to mind when I remember her east European accent and something the French call *je ne sais quoi*. Was it a refinement or sophistication I was unused to that made her special? I don't know, but she was different from the girls we had grown up with. Did Scott attract her like a flame? Like honey? Was *he* exotic to her? I don't know that either, but as a younger, aspiring Romeo, I was curious. I knew his natural charm must have been part of the equation, but I was interested in the details. Of course, I didn't ask.

I'm struck now by the irony of the spark that flashed between Scott and Lena. He was the great grandson of Santino Fontana, a granite cutter who subscribed to Luigi Galleani's anarchist newspaper, and died of stone dust in his lungs at thirty-nine. She

---

[5] The names of most of the girls in this chapter have been changed out of a regard for privacy.

was the niece of a wealthy European financier who died in his seventies swimming under an azure sky in the blue waters of the Caribbean. The disparity between Scott's origins and Lena's was wide. Ah—young lovers do not care if their parents sit in the same pew on Sundays. I guess Scott and Lena's brief romance can be filed under the heading of an "experience the Hastings brothers would not have imagined" before moving to Woodstock.

One of Scott's other girlfriends I remember even better. I'll call her Venus. I often sat across a lunch table from her in Dorothy Cook's study hall when I was a freshman. She was a sweet brunette with wavy hair, soft eyes, a womanly figure even as a teen, and a slight lisp. She was a junior at the time and a varsity cheerleader. We traveled on the same school bus when the Woodstock Wasps basketball team went to away games, but we never sat together. The ball players could not sit with the cheerleaders, and anyway, I was a lowly freshman boy and she was a junior. The gulf between us was wide and deep, to say nothing of the fact that she was going out with my brother.

Somehow, she had obtained a copy of *Fanny Hill*, a book first published in 1748, and not published legally until 1963. She showed me the tasteful cover one day in study hall, and at first, I wondered why she was reading a classic. She quietly slid the book across the table, indicated a certain passage and warned me not to attract Mrs. Cook's attention. I read the detailed description and found it not only enlightening but also stimulating. Really stimulating. The subtitle, by the way, was *Memoirs of a Woman of Pleasure.* When the bell surprised me at the end of study hall, I had to take my time packing up my books and let the cafeteria clear before I could leave without embarrassment.

Scott's male friends were, like him, some of the smartest guys in his class. Jim Roberts and Pete Sawyer were on the football team, and Scott was disappointed that *he* couldn't play. Unfortunately for Scott—or perhaps fortunately—a player in nearby Windsor had recently suffered a football injury that put him in a wheelchair for life. That was that. Mom and Dad said football was out. It was a blow, but he accepted the decision gracefully as far I could tell. He found other ways to amuse himself. Jim, Pete, Rick Harding, and Scott became good friends during high school, partly, I think, because of a shared interest in hi-jinks. By the time they became seniors, they had a well-established reputation for humorous stunts and unconventional thinking. Rick Harding's senior quote for the yearbook was typical: "It is my solemn belief that the ape is descended from Man."

For some reason, one of their milder exploits stands out. Let me set the stage. It is the first day of school in September, 1966. Woodstock Union High School is a Division 2 school, not especially big, but for many students coming from the small schools of Bridgewater and other nearby towns, it is a first experience with something that might be called institutional. Students are spilling out of buses parked along the circular drive at the front of the school. They enter the main corridor through doors at either end of the unloading area and go directly to the gym where they find seats in the bleachers. If they are sophomores, juniors, or seniors, they look for their friends. If they are freshmen, they glance warily about for anyone they might know, or they sit by themselves and hope to survive their first day of high school.

Suddenly, *brrrrrinnnnngg!* It's the first bell, and you have five minutes to get to your homeroom where you will hear the morning announcements. Just over four hundred students flow out of the gym like lemmings and through the double doors into the hallway of the academic wing. The hallway becomes crowded and a little rowdy. A din of voices, clanging lockers, clattering shoes, and shouted greetings creates an air of excitement. What will this new school year bring? Imagine now, that you are halfway down the corridor standing with a couple good friends as I was. You are comparing class schedules, asking about the new English teacher with the southern accent, Mr. Turner, bemoaning the fact that your parents are making you take Latin with Miss Jollivete, and wondering if you will pass her class because she is a *hard* teacher, and then—you hear something. It is muffled at first because it is happening beyond the closing-and-opening double doors at the far end of the hall where a few students are still entering from the gym.

And then the dam bursts. The doors fly open, and Jim, Scott, and Pete charge through like firemen on their way to a burning building. They are pulling Rick Harding in a red wagon and slalom down the hall and between the clusters of students fast enough to avoid the teachers who suddenly appear in their doorways to see what all the fuss is about. They race to the far end of the wing where they are placed in handcuffs and taken into custody. Well, I'm exaggerating about the cuffs, but they are definitely called to the office and given detentions. I'm sure each of them wore his disgrace like Stephen Crane's red badge of courage which they had learned about in Miss Ridlon's English class. They weren't the role models the administration wanted them to be, but they were the heroes of the day for us underclassmen.

Duncan was twelve and in sixth grade when we moved to town. His school friends Bob Millen and Jay Morgan were now neighbors. The Millens lived nearby in the house with the turret on the corner of High Street. Dunc and Bob quickly discovered they both loved to fish and prepared their first Kedron Brook expedition. Late one afternoon they gathered worms, extra hooks, and a couple candy bars. Then, they slipped around the fence behind our house and began their leisurely progress upstream. They cast their lines into likely pools with little luck. By the time they reached the "No Trespassing" and "No Fishing" signs posted at the property line of the Woodstock Country Club, Duncan had landed a meager seven-inch trout. Bob was skunked. The day was dwindling and dusk was bringing shadows. They looked at each other.

"I bet there's some good pools up ahead," said Bob.

"Yeah. And the Country Club stocks the brook."

"Let's go."

A decision made so easily bodes well for friendship. Clearly, they were kindred spirits. They continued upstream, now moving stealthily. Dad told us once that Robin Hood might have been one of our ancestors. Dunc decided that if his forefather Robin dared to poach the King's deer in Sherwood Forest, he and Bob could risk taking a few trout from Mr. Rockefeller's preserve, perhaps under the very noses of one or two avid golfers still clubbing little white balls up and down the fairways in the waning light. Finally, his compass veered from true north. Staying low and blending in with the tall grass lining the brook's banks, they snagged a few trout in the ten to twelve-inch range. Ah—fish for breakfast! Always tasty fried in egg batter.

But the best was yet to come. They found their pot of gold when they reached a spot where golfers had to hit across the brook. It was another one of those unanticipated opportunities Mom had sensed but couldn't put a name to when she gave her pep talk on moving to town. Bob was staring down into a pool and Dunc followed his gaze. Golf balls were keeping the trout company at the bottom of the Kedron. Lots of golf balls. The two outlaws sloshed into the brook and filled their pockets. It's a great thing about being a kid—you don't care if you get wet. As they worked their way upstream, always wary, always furtive, they found more. Some of the balls sat by themselves, waiting hopefully in the mud for the next slug of rain that would push them downstream again in a faster current. Some had tumbled along until the current petered out and stranded them in an eddy with others of their kind, clustered like eggs in a nest.

Why the excitement over a few golf balls? Money! Filthy lucre, as Dad sometimes called it. Scott had caddied at the club, and Bob's dad played golf, so Dunc and Bob were aware that they had stumbled on the golden golf ball goose. Balls were expensive at the Pro Shop, and these intrepid golf ball fishermen knew that local guys would love to buy Top Flites and Titleists at discount prices. Mr. Millen put out the word, and because word travels fast, our modern-day merry men became entrepreneurs overnight.

When they weren't fishing for fish and golf balls in the Kedron or riding their bicycles to Barnard with their snorkeling gear to spearfish for perch or catfish, Bob, Dunc, and Jay joined the legions of kids who gathered at Vail Field whenever the weather allowed. Henry H. Vail gave the field to the Town of Woodstock in 1895, and its use for baseball, circus performances, and all manner of entertainment for the town was written into the deed. The baseball diamond, weather-beaten grandstand, and bandstand were still there when we were growing up, and an outdoor basketball court and a couple tennis courts had been added as well. Kids came from all over town to play ball. Rusty Morgan, Morgan Vail, Jeff West, Robin Dayman, and Pat Donahue were regular Vail Field gladiators in Dunc's age group. They played baseball, softball, flag football, and basketball depending on the season and the number of guys present.

There were also after-hour sports at Vail Field. One evening after the sun had gone down, and the shadows were disappearing into darkness, a father who lived in proximity to Vail Field was crossing the dewy grass near home plate on his way to the footbridge across the Kedron. It was a warm, pleasant summer evening, the kind of evening when, as a younger man, he might have been lucky enough to enjoy the company of a girl. He might have even been lucky enough to be encouraged by her in that co-ed sport that has been called a various times spooning or sparking or necking.

Passing close to the grandstand and remembering, perhaps, such a pleasant time from his youth, he was startled back into the present by whispers. Deciding to investigate, he found his lovely twelve-year-old daughter—let's call her Belle—making out with that upstart Duncan Hastings, the youngest son of that oddball who played the bagpipes on Golf Avenue. Duncan had recently given Belle a charm bracelet, and his charms were working well. Belle's Dad was livid. He raked Dunc over the coals, promising grave

Duncan's senior picture. No Brylcreem. Sideburns!

---

consequences if he ever found him with his daughter again, and then he stormed away with Belle in tow. That night's chance for sport on Vail Field was sadly interrupted, but the story was not done.

The rudely interrupted tryst between Duncan

and Belle happened during the summer of 1967. Within a matter of weeks, we moved again, this time to Flagstaff, Arizona. Dad had received a grant from the Ford Foundation to study anthropology at Northern Arizona University, and we were to spend the '67/68' school year in the land of the Navaho, the horned toad, and the Grand Canyon. Scott was enrolled at the University of Vermont and would stay with Gram and Gramp during school vacations. We packed up, Duncan did not see his Belle before we left town, and a possible brawl between the Capulets and Montagues was averted.

Duncan was looking forward to renewing his acquaintance with Belle on his return and was thinking of ways to smooth her father's ruffled feathers, and—if that failed—thinking of ways to circumvent him. In similar fashion, Belle was looking forward to seeing Duncan again and hearing exciting stories about life in the West, about cowboys, and about whether the girls there were really wearing shirts with pearl buttons and fringes, and more importantly, she was also thinking about ways to butter up her dad and convince him that Duncan was really a nice young man who had no intention of "moving too fast."

But when Duncan came home, the unexpected happened. He received a message from one of his classmates that Belle did not wish to see him again. Ever. The girl who contacted Dunc was only the messenger. She was sent by another girl—let's relegate her to anonymity—and that girl had a crush on Dunc. This gives you some insight into my other brother's powers of attraction. He had a different style than Scott, but his Jimmy Dean good looks (ears notwithstanding), earnest manner, and winning smile could charm the pants off—well, never mind. The upshot was that Duncan and Belle never picked up where they left off that night on Vail Field. Holy hotcakes! Who knows what might have happened if they had? Belle thought Duncan had been scared off by her father. Duncan thought Belle wanted nothing to do with him. Not knowing about the unnamed girl's scheming, he dated her briefly, but of course, the sly minx wasn't his type. And afterwards, like mine, his high school years were a desert with only an occasional oasis when it came to romance. It was decades later that he and Belle finally discovered the truth about the plot to keep them apart. It makes me wonder. How much of this play we call life happens behind the scenes?

 I said *my* high school years were also a desert when it came to romance. I had hoped a girl I'll call Deidre would cure my lovelorn longings, but it was not meant to be. You may think she was put off when I tossed popcorn at the back of her head while sitting behind her with Fred Doubleday watching Alfred Hitchcock's *Rear Window* when we were in sixth grade. I admit it was dumb. She forgave me, and we were always friendly, but it was quite clearly a case of unrequited love. The last nail was driven into that romantic coffin on a fall day soon after I started my freshman year at the high school. An upperclassman named Buck (not really) was now Deidre's boyfriend. I was mystified by her attraction to him. Maybe it had to do with his maroon Ford convertible with the rumbling V-8 engine.

That day he was just pulling away from the curb out in front of the school with the top down and lovely Deidre in the passenger seat. From my place on the dung heap of discarded admirers, a crazy impulse took control and lifted my hand in a one-finger salute. Buck had an impulse too. He saw my salute in his rearview mirror, backed up surprisingly quickly, vaulted out of the car, and punched me in the face. I stood there stunned as he jumped back in the girlmobile and sped away with squealing tires in a final display of power. I turned sixteen shades of crimson and told my hand not to be so impulsive in the future. There were onlookers, of course, and the news spread. If possible, my status as a lowly freshman dropped even lower, and I had to be on my guard with bullies who would now see me as easy pickin's, but nothing much really happened. I had been put in my place.

Deciding that further courting of Deidre was foolhardy, I thought of Deborah Belden, the new girl from Pico. Would she go out with me? I had met her at our last eighth grade dance in the spring. I had crossed the wooden floor in Woodstock's Little Theater, and asked her for the last dance. It was a slow dance. She put her hand on my shoulder, smiled sweetly, and allowed me to hold her in my arms. By the end of the dance, I was again in love. Remembering that night and noticing again in Miss Ridlon's English class that she was quite attractive—she was prom queen two years later—I talked to my friend Fred Doubleday who seemed to know her already.

"Do you think Deb Belden would go out with me?"

"She's already going steady with Tom Barrup." So—I think you get the picture. My love life was pretty unexciting for the next few years. Rock Taylor's girlfriend Ginny Cleaver adopted me for the night of July Fourth that next summer. I don't know where Rock was, and in spite of my experience with Buck, I didn't care, which shows the extent of my frustration because Rock was a Bridgewater boy, and those mill town kids had a reputation for being tough. I didn't even hold hands with Ginny that night. But she too was sweet, and I remember it as a wonderful evening even if it was—unfortunately—all quite platonic. The only real excitement was when one of the Lions Club's rockets spiraled through the crowd.

About the time Duncan was regretfully saying goodbye to Belle on Vail Field, I was saying goodbye to Diane Gulick on the shores of a lake near Camp Rising Sun in Rhinebeck, New York. I was sixteen and had just spent the summer with boys from all over the world: Italy, Great Britain, Japan, Turkey, and so on. The camper from Turkey could walk on his hands and move a soccer ball with his feet like no one I'd ever seen. Hannu Pekka-Lappalainen from Finland looked like Captain Kangaroo but had W.C. Fields' sense of humor. Giuseppe Niccolini from Rome was—by his account, at least—the quintessential lady's man.

It was a great summer, a summer of experiments. I was introduced to the blues by counselor Phil Terry. Phil played the fiddle, and we got up one morning and did a bagpipe-fiddle duet to rouse the camp. Boy, did we rouse everyone. I played the part of the Police Sergeant when Camp Rising Sun put on *The Pirates of Penzance*. I had to sing—in public! And act! Unheard

Alec's senior picture. Brylcreem or Vitalis still in use.

of! But even though I had a blast teasing Mama Glen while working in her kitchen, learning about Plato from Sandy Dennis while seated under a catalpa tree, and visiting the Metropolitan Museum of Art in the City of Cities, it was a summer where girl sightings were rare. You can imagine my joy upon hearing that the boys of Camp Rising Sun were to visit the girls of Camp Delmar on the last day of the season. It was a tradition and one I was glad to uphold. I was so very happy to make the acquaintance of Miss Gulick on Delmar Day. Diane was blonde and beautiful, smart and funny. We kissed. It was over fifty years ago, but I still remember the breathless excitement, the gratitude for that fleeting moment with a mermaid.

And then, in the wingbeat of a butterfly, Delmar Day was over. Back home at the end of the summer, I said goodbye to Fred and Bill. Then, the Hastings family—minus brother Scott—headed for Big Sky Country, the famed American West we had seen so many times on *Rawhide* and *Gunsmoke*. At Flagstaff High, I went to school for the first time with African Americans, Asian Americans, Navahos, Hopis, Mormons, Mexican Americans, and the descendants of Dust Bowl refugees. And for the first time in my life, *I* was "the new kid." It was time, finally, to shape up or ship out.

We took fitness tests during the first week of gym class. I ran the 100-yard dash and the 440 with good times—enough to mildly impress a few of my classmates. Shortly after finishing, however, I went to the locker room and threw up. I was a little confused about why this happened since I wasn't in a car on a winding Vermont road. Even if I had been in a car, all the roads around Flagstaff were straight and flat. This was when I learned about rarefied air. I knew by this time that humans need oxygen to live. I didn't know that a Vermont kid like me, used to the oxygen-rich air of Woodstock (elevation 700 feet above sea level) was going to find significantly less O_2 in Flagstaff (el. 7,000 feet) and that the discrepancy would amount to six, twisty, "please hand me the upchuck bag" Vermont roads. Later, I learned that Olympic athletes train in Flagstaff because running at 7,000 feet develops stamina. I wish someone had told me about rarefied air earlier. Maybe I could have talked my gym teacher into letting me become acclimated to Flagstaff's higher altitude before being tested. But then, remembering that teacher, I realize this would have been a vain hope.

Two months later, that same teacher, the hulking, six-foot-six ex-football player, Mr. Johnson, started us on a week of wrestling. To my own surprise, I kind of liked Coach Johnson. One reason I did was because he didn't put me up against Booker, the heavily-muscled black kid who, cheerful as he was, would have flung me down and pinned me to the mat in seconds without a moment's concern for my reputation. Instead, Coach Johnson matched me with a guy of my own slender build, Hobbs or Hobby as he was called. The class had been practicing wrestling holds and moves for days, and to my surprise as much as anyone else's, I had mastered them. I threw Hobby to the mat as forcefully as if I were Haystack Calhoun, the six-hundred pound wrestler who became one of our favorite costumed, theatrical contenders when my brothers and I joined Gramp to watch televised wrestling on Saturday afternoons back home. In fact, I threw Hobby to the mat the way Booker would have thrown me. What a lousy moral compass I had.

I could tell by the quizzical expression on Coach Johnson's face that he thought my lightning-strike victory was a fluke. He immediately matched me against Rick. Rick was, again, my height, but a little heavier, a little stronger, and a little quicker than Hobby. *Bam!* The same thing happened. I slammed him to the mat and knocked the wind out of him. I had a new nickname after that—Crippler. Maybe the rarefied air was turning me into a wrestling prodigy, and The Crippler would become my super hero, comic book name.

But the new nickname didn't get me a girlfriend,

and in a school of well over a thousand students, my notoriety was minimal and short-lived. Anyone in my classes who was even remotely interested in "the new kid" soon learned I was headed home at the end of the school year. Why spend time getting to know a guy who is going to disappear in June like the snow on the San Francisco Peaks just outside town? So, I sat with Rudy Contraris at lunch every day, ate my peanut butter and jelly sandwich, watched him eat his bean taco, and observed the placid stream of teen life flow past. Well, it was a placid stream most of the time, but I was reminded once again there was often more going on around me than met the eye. Events in the main corridor one morning made this especially clear. Two black girls got into a fight over a boy when everyone was changing classes. They screamed—using colorful language I wasn't sure Dad even knew—raked each other with fingernails, pulled hair, and tore each other's blouses half off. Whew! How fast the usually placid stream could become a raging torrent!

Most days, however, the current of life moved along lazily. Rudy was a Mexican American who always wore a white shirt and black pants as if he were headed to church. He was a good guy, but he was kind of an outsider. Like me. Being an outsider was another valuable learning experience. I began to realize, for instance, that I really *could* stand on my own two feet and be—in my fantasy world, at least—like Gary Cooper who stood up to the Miller gang in *High Noon* even though a drunk and a kid and finally his wife were the only people who backed him.

After school every day, Duncan and I returned to our one-story cinder block housing at the Northern Arizona University Museum just outside town. There we found the only thing that mattered—home, which really just meant Mom and Dad. At dinner Dunc told stories about a short, eighth-grade African American classmate named Carlos Natt, who apparently looked like an anteater. On the first day of school, Carlos had a question for Dunc.

"Where you from, boy?"

"Vermont."

"What state dat in?"

I'm not sure how Duncan answered. It may have taken him a moment to formulate a tactful reply. Carlos Natt. It was an unfortunate last name, but he was an interesting character, and Duncan's accounts of their conversations not only entertained us, but also reminded us we were not in Kansas anymore—or Vermont. After supper, Dunc and I would go outside. More than once, Mom questioned us about our activities.

"What are you going to do out there? It's getting dark."

"Nothing," we replied in unison. "Just walk around, get a little exercise."

"Nothing," of course, meant *something*, something verging on the illicit or risky, something requiring an ability to misread one's inner compass. I remember, for instance, the night of our first mission as secret agents. Yes, we *were* a little old to be playing such games, but, hey, we were desperate for a little fun. We first thought of becoming spies when we noticed a solid-looking drain pipe at the corner of one of the research buildings. We shinnied up the pipe, crept stealthily across the roof, and became—for a few brave moments of self-delusion—Napoleon Solo and Illya Kuryakin, the spies from the T.V. series, *Man from U.N.C.L.E.* Right away, our ability to blend chameleon-like into the shadows was tested. A purring engine signaled the appearance of a car. Headlights swept across the compound. It was the rent-a-cops! We glanced at each other in silent agreement, dashed toward the gap between our building and the next, and leaped! Did they see us? No. We were too fast, too clever by half.

I think back on those night missions and our other Arizona adventures and am grateful I had Duncan's company for that long school year spent in exile. He really showed his mettle at the Battle of Mule Deer Mountain. We had been hiking all morning across a hot little chunk of desert on our way to the foothills of the San Francisco Peaks, and had just reached a hillside clearing where we were about to eat lunch. Suddenly, Duncan's hand darted to his World War I bayonet. The blade flashed, and quicker than Zorro, he swung it down. Wow! There at my feet was the severed head of a snake.

Yes, I was grateful for his company, although to be fair to the snake, it wasn't a rattler as he first suspected. It *was*, however, most definitely dead, and as we looked uneasily around, we saw we were surrounded. We stood in the middle of a convention of snakes who, until that moment, had been peacefully and lazily tanning themselves in the warm glade. Now, alert, uneasy, and understandably unhappy about the loss of their comrade, they stared at us with beady eyes and flicked their tongues as we tiptoed back to the safety of the trees. Yeah, I was glad for Dunc's company that year. He and I were The Two Musketeers, and we managed to scrape up some fun even in the desolate wastes of the vast Southwest.

Mom and Dad helped with that as well. They were good parents who knew weekend excursions would give all of us something exciting to look forward to during the week and something memorable to look back on even decades later. We ventured off to mysterious Indian ruins and historic sites that whispered of the past, places like Wupatki Canyon, Walnut Canyon, and Hoskinini Mesa. We visited Sunset Crater, Glen Canyon Dam, and the Navaho and Hopi Reservations where we saw mule deer, coyotes, road runners, tree lizards, and snakes. Yes, more snakes. We saw cacti, lots and lots of cacti. We saw geological formations—buttes, mesas, and canyons—that were millions of years old. One day we grew puzzled gazing at a white dot drifting far below us in the vast abyss of the Grand Canyon. What was it? Finally, we figured it out. A helicopter! It seemed impossibly far away. Dad and I got our pipes out of the car and played a couple tunes there on the rim of one of the world's most awe-inspiring wonders.

All these years later, I realize the summer at Camp Rising Sun and the school year at Flagstaff High helped me grow up. I *did* miss my friends at times, but when I returned to Woodstock, I had changed, and it was for the better. Maybe the march through the desert was coming to an end. I joined the W.U.H.S. Student Council, became a yearbook editor, and played on the Wasps basketball team. Now, one of the "unimagined

Alec and Dad piping at the Grand Canyon, 1967 or '68.

experiences" Mom talked about was coming *my* way. I went to a statewide student gathering at Windham College in Putney. It was the spring of '69. The concert at Woodstock, New York was only a few months away. Most of the students at Windham, like those at Goddard College, opposed the Vietnam War and were politically active. I suppose they organized the gathering of high school students to raise the students' awareness of the war, civil rights, and women's liberation. All this was lost on me. I was aware only of a beautiful girl named Luanne. She was a student from Hartford High, and—she was the first flower child I ever met.

We saw each other again after we returned home to the Upper Valley. I had my driver's license and borrowed the family car to visit her at an old farmhouse on the road between Sharon and South Strafford. She was living with a hip high school teacher and his wife, but they weren't around. Luanne met me at the door wearing a peasant blouse and faded bell bottom jeans. Did she have flowers in her hair? I know it sounds like a cliché now, but I think she did, and if she didn't, that's still the way I remember her. Did she go to the concert on Max Yasgur's farm that summer, the one they called Woodstock? Maybe. We might have listened to Joni Mitchell's *Clouds* or Dylan's *Nashville Skyline*. They had just been released. Ours was another one-day romance, and she was another mermaid who allowed me to come close. I have appreciated flowers ever since.

❖

The Undiscovered Country

Epilogue

Endings are hard for me. I'm sure I'm not alone in this. Whether I'm saying goodbye to a friend or goodbye to a reader, and when the occasion requires more than a wave and a "Hi-yo, Silver, away!" I sometimes feel as if the right words are *not* on the tip of my tongue. Instead, they are dancing a jig in the yard and thumbing their noses at me.

At such times I resign myself to the task of thinking *hard* about what to say. Thinking hard is not my forte, you see. I'm a storyteller, not a philosopher. Also, I'm easily distracted. Even now, just thinking about thinking hard, I am distracted by the memory of Tom Terrific, a cartoon character on *Captain Kangaroo*, a children's T.V. show in the late 1950s. I picture the puzzled Tom sitting on a stump with his magical thinking-cap funnel on his head, smoke pouring from his ears. He is wrestling with a knotty problem, and then—"Eureka!"—he says and solves it. I wish I had a magic, thinking-cap funnel.

I must have wished for Tom's cap three times

because, just as in the fairy tales, I suddenly felt the cold metal of a large funnel atop my head. Heat rose in my chest and I became breathless. I felt flushed, and then I smelled the first whiff of smoke just like Tommy T. As the smoke tickled my nose, I tapped on a door in my brain and was invited to enter the special room where eureka moments happen if one thinks really hard.

I heard a distant yodel from the prologue. I was transported back to Happy Valley, to the pine tree Scott had climbed, the one I climbed after him. Once again, I rose from a crouch, tentatively tall and proud. I cupped my hands around my mouth and let loose the call of the jungle. Again, my voice was swallowed by the forest. But something was different this time. I was not disappointed. As a boy, I had wanted my voice to travel from one end of Happy Valley to the other. Now, nearing seventy, I no longer cared to make my mark, to say "I am here."

This kind of turnabout has happened to me a number of times. Often, I have been sure about something only to find myself wrong or in need of a course correction. You may, for instance, remember the time I found gold in the Gully only to learn it was fool's gold. This is why I am so often skeptical of certainty in myself or in others. I was not entirely

Epilogue

surprised, then, when *Cap Pistols* became something more than what I thought it would be. I thought it would be just a home movie on paper, a collection stories for family and anyone nostalgic about a vanished Vermont.

For me, it became something more. I worked for months on these stories, and when my old friend serendipity showed up, the book became one of the cereal boxes I used to open as a kid, the kind with a surprise inside. The surprise was that, *in tinkering with the past, I changed it.* I know I sound like an oddball in a science fiction movie, the guy who believes he can go back in time and affect the outcome of the Civil War or prevent the assassination of President Kennedy.

I don't mean I literally changed the past, of course. I mean that all the resurrection of the past, the conversations with my brothers, the summoning of ghosts, the retelling of stories brought me a *new version* of the past. The grown-ups of my youth are no longer giants towering over me, but paradoxically, many of them have even greater stature now. Writing this book was like turning the adjuster on a pair of high-powered binoculars. Even though sixty years have passed—probably *because* sixty years have passed—I see my parents and grandparents more clearly, and—

warts and all—I am more grateful than ever for the upbringing they gave me.

It has occurred to me that memoirs often dig into the middens of personal history and unearth prosaic bits and bobs that—examined in the right light—turn out be treasures, gems of wisdom, or keys to mysteries. Uncovering and studying even one memory can lead to discovery. Time and again, Scott or Duncan or I would describe an event or a person we remembered, and that memory would spark another, and then another. Most of the time, we shared similar versions of the past, but sometimes we remembered completely different versions or different details or felt differently about what happened. I learned new things about the people I knew long ago, about what made them tick, and—by extension—what made me tick, what makes me tick. I felt a new gratitude for the glowing presence of the people who first acquainted me with the wide world.

I won't catalog all the ways my parents and grandparents put their stamp on me, but here are a few. When I asked Gramp why his fingers were a little crooked, he told me he had caught them between heavy steel rollers at the paper mill. The doctor wanted to amputate. Gramp wouldn't hear of it. With mutterings about blood poisoning, the doctor

Epilogue

finally agreed. While Gramp bit down on a round of wood, the doc cleaned the raw, mashed fingers with a vegetable brush and iodine, and then he bandaged them. Gramp kept the fingers after all. For me, he was the epitome of a man who had sand. I don't know that I ever heard him complain about an ailment. I try to follow in his footsteps in this regard, but I confess I am not his match.

Mom and I had our differences in later years—probably, because we were so much alike—but when my brothers and I were boys, she was the best of mothers. She laughed with us, loved us, and at the same time explained to us the importance of good manners, kindness, cleanliness, and responsibility which she also taught by example. Woe to the boy who did not wash his hands before coming to the table, was mean to a poor, dumb animal, or made rude noises in church. Although failing sometimes—especially with the cleanliness—I did my best to learn these traits as a boy and have continued to uphold them as a grown up.

If any of the folks set a high bar for accomplishment, it was Dad. He could build just about anything from wood. He made bagpipes, boats, tables, chairs, beds, our house—you name it. His idea of a midlife crisis was to apply for a Ford Foundation grant, study anthropology at a university in Arizona, and come home and write books about Vermont folklore. I'm certainly grateful for the example he provided, but I'm even more grateful that—with us—he was just our dad, a guy who loved and cared about us.

And that brings me to two people I have always dearly loved but whose *full* impact on me has been something I discovered only while writing this book. As I grow old myself and look back on my boyhood, I always remember Gram and Elmer Bumps with great affection. For me, they radiated simple love and joy like a kitchen stove radiates heat, a steady, sustaining, comforting warmth. I feel it even now. They were completely unassuming. They never stood out for their accomplishments. They never put themselves forward. They lived with a simplicity of spirit Thoreau might have envied. For sixty years my memory of the kind way they acted toward others has guided me. Their presence has always been reassuring. I have continued to learn from their example even though I remember only one spoken bit of advice.

It came from Gram. "If you smile," she said, "even if you are unhappy and don't feel like smiling, you will soon feel better, and your smile will become real." How simple. Some might say, too simple, and dismiss the words and the speaker. I have remembered Gram's

Epilogue

advice always, not solely for the words themselves, but for the way I saw her and Elmer embody them daily. They had a remarkable intelligence of the heart. I have aspired to that kind of intelligence all my life. It was not and is not easy, and I fail often. To let go of my self, to be as kind and happy and generous as it is in my capacity to be—this is my aim. This is the treasure I carried with me from Happy Valley.

ACKNOWLEDGEMENTS

With love in my heart, I want to acknowledge my daughters' gift. I had no idea just how wonderful a project *Cap Pistrols, Cardboard Sleds & Seven Rusty Nails* would become. Thank you Calley Hastings, Katie Amadon, and Josey Archdeacon for assigning this task and even for making me think hard now and again! If you hadn't signed me up for Storyworth, who knows if I would ever have written this? I hope you and others enjoy these stories from Happy Valley.

Every week for a few months, I talked with my brothers Scott and Duncan about this memoir, about our shenanigans as kids, and especially about the people we grew up with. Sometimes they had a different perspective on people and events, and sometimes they remembered things I didn't. Our collective remembering helped me return to the scenes of our youth, and often I saw those scenes more clearly and completely with my brothers' help. I found our phone visits entertaining and enlightening. I was surprised that after sixty years we could resurrect the past in so much detail. Perhaps we could do so because we listened to our elders do the same once upon a time. *Cap Pistrols, Cardboard Sleds & Seven Rusty Nails* is surely a better book because of our conversations. I am grateful, guys.

From time to time, I looked to other writers for inspiration. I reread parts of Dad's book, *Goodbye Highland Yankee*. I did the same with *The Story of a Bad Boy* by Thomas Bailey Aldrich, a book given to Dad for Christmas by his father's sister, Aunt Eunice, probably in the 1930s when he was near the age of the story's narrator. I also reread parts of Bruce Coffin's 2020 memoir, *Among Familiar Shadows*. Bruce grew up in Woodstock as I did, but I loved his book not just because he wrote of places I knew, but because he wrote in such a revelatory way about the people he knew, people who became as familiar as my own family. I liked his book so much I used an excerpt from it as an epigraph for this one. I am particularly grateful for Bruce's help with this manuscript. His copy editing netted many errors, and his urging for revision of the ending gave me the nudge I needed to dig down for better work. There is no doubt that *Cap Pistrols, Cardboard Sleds & Seven Rusty Nails* benefited significantly from his generous help. Thank you, Bruce.

Acknowledgements

My mainstay, my lodestar in writing this book was my wife, Denise Martin. As always, she listened to me read new installments aloud at our kitchen table, and somehow she always found the perfect balance between encouragement and honest critique in her responses. She knows and can name specifically what she might question, what I might need to consider and perhaps revise. Like Bruce, she saw that the first ending of the book was not what it could be. Neither was the second. This is the process, of course. Keep thinking, keep writing, and rewriting, and with a little luck, the hoped-for work will emerge. *Grazie, mia cara, per tutto il tuo aiuto!*

Finally, I think of Carrie Cook as I send *Cap Pistols, Cardboard Sleds & Seven Rusty Nails* out to the world. She is a friend and a most expert designer of books. Pleasing fonts and a well-proportioned layout are a big part of what make a book beautiful. Thank you, Carrie, for making the words in this book wear their Sunday best!

◆

www.ingramcontent.com/pod-product-compliance
Lightning Source LLC
Chambersburg PA
CBHW051557010526
44118CB00023B/2735